FORTY MORE
PUB W
IN SURREY

Forty Circular Walks

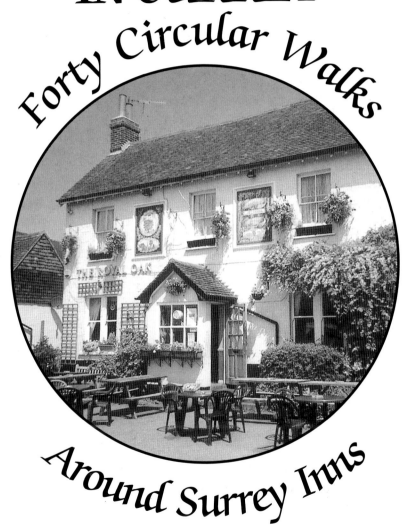

Around Surrey Inns

John Quarendon

Other publications in the series
"Pub Walks in Dorset"
"Forty More Pub Walks in Dorset"
"Pub Walks in Somerset"
"Pub Walks in West Sussex"
"Pub Walks in East Sussex"
"Pub Walks in Kent"
"Pub Walks in Hants & the IOW"
"Pub Walks in Devon"
"Pub Walks in Cornwall"
"Pub Walks in the New Forest"
"Pub Walks in Hardy's Wessex"
"Mike Power's Pub Walks Along the Dorset Coast"
"Pub Walks in North Surrey"
"Pub Walks in South Surrey"

1st edition published 2005

Acknowledgements
Thanks once again to my wife Margaret, who trod every mile and proof read and to my daughter Suzy, who typed up all my notes.

© John Quarendon

ISBN 1898073317

Power Publications
1 Clayford Ave
Ferndown, Dorset.
BH22 9PQ
sales@powerpublications.co.uk

Publishers note:
Whilst every care has been taken to ensure that all the information contained in this book is correct neither the author nor the publisher can accept any responsibility for any inaccuracies that might occur.

Printed by Pardy & Son (Printers) Ltd, Ringwood, Hants.
Front cover: The Royal Oak, Brockham.
Layout: Mike Power.
Photographs and drawings : John Quarendon.

2

Introduction

Researching the earlier two books – Forty Pub Walks in North Surrey and Forty Pub Walks in South Surrey – left me with a thirst to explore yet more of this beautiful county. It transpired that I had left some of the best walks with superb views and stunning bluebell woods, and some of the best pubs until last. The success of the other books, both still available, encouraged the publishers to take a third volume. So keen pub walkers can now obtain a comprehensive guide to the county's best footpaths in 120 circular walks, many of them intersecting to provide the option of longer rambles and all for under £15.

The Walks

The Walks are circular between 3½ and 6 miles and designed to start and finish at the featured pub. Thirty of the walks intersect with others to give the option of longer rambles of 7-10 miles. Alternative free parking facilities en route are indicated on the maps with the letter P and nearby railway stations are also indicated. The maps are generally in proportion but not precisely to scale. You can usually get away with summer walking in trainers but on Surrey's heavy soils I strongly recommend walking boots at other times or where the walk description warns of mud. Footpaths are often poorly maintained and long trousers offer protection against nettles, brambles and insects. A walking stick is a useful aid on overgrown paths and, when raised, seems to act as a deterrent to over inquisitive heifers. An Ordnance Survey, Explorer Series, 1:25000 map, a compass, Swiss army knife, antihistamine bite/sting treatment, compact binoculars and compact camera are useful walking companions and should all fit into a decent sized bum bag.

The format of the Forty Walks series is designed to give maximum value for money in terms of the number of walks. It does not allow space for much background information, so the main landmarks and places of historical interest are only referred to in passing. For the same reason the bird watching notes are restricted to the more unusual sightings.

The Pubs

In those cases where a choice of pubs was available on the planned route the selection criteria were choice of real ales and wines, appetising original menus with snacks and main meals, stressing the use of fresh ingredients and home cooking, value for money, low volume of any music and separation of amusements from the dining area. Ambience is important and the sort of welcome you get when you approach the bar. As I know to my cost it is sensible to check if the pub is still open before travelling and also to book in advance for parties, particularly on Sundays. Please ask permission before parking to walk. Pubs are constantly changing hands, changing character or being closed down. If what you find here is not what you find there, you will know that another one has bitten the dust in the interval between the writing and the walking.

The Country Code

Please keep to footpaths, shut all gates, damage no property, light no fires, dig no bulbs, leave no litter and keep dogs on leads near livestock. Kiss at all kissing gates if suitably accompanied. If not hang about for the U3A party coming along behind. Somebody's granny/grandad might make your day.

Surrey
Map of
Walk Locations

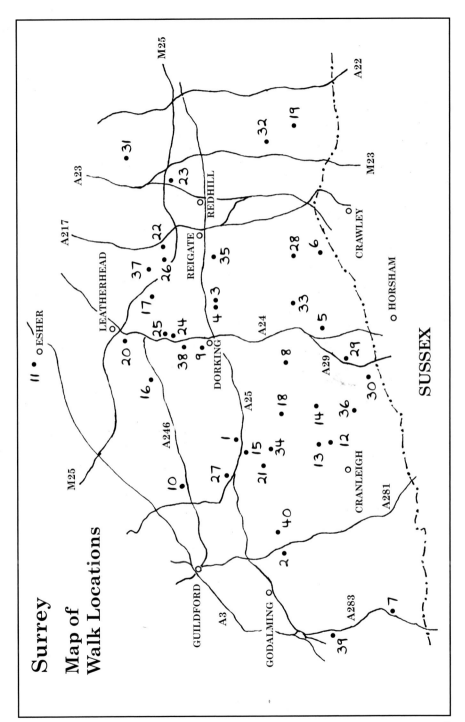

The Abinger Arms, Abinger Hammer.

The Abinger Arms, on a corner site opposite the famous Abinger Hammer clock, is popular with the many 'Pilgrims' walking their Way and The North Downs Way and dropping down to the nearest hostelry for refreshment.

On our visit the ales were limited to Marstons Pedigree and Youngs Bitter but this was compensated for by a comprehensive and imaginative menu and friendly service.

The usual snacks of baguettes, jackets and ploughman's are available along with daily specials like roast pheasant, haunch of venison, shoulder of lamb, poached salmon and homemade patés, soups, burgers and pies. Fish and chips and curries are also available as takeaways. If you are in a de-tox programme "traditional afternoon tea" could replace the traditional alcoholic lunch as the pub is open all day every day from 11am, Sun 12 noon. In addition to the lounge bar there are smoking and non smoking dining areas with log fires in winter and a beer garden at the rear.

Children and dogs are welcome.

Tel: 01306 730145.

The Abinger Arms is on the A25 at the junction with Hackhurst Lane in the centre of Abinger Hammer. There is limited parking at the pub or at Abinger Roughs National Trust car park – see map. The walk passes close to Gomshall railway station.

Approx distance of walk 5 miles. Start at OS Map Ref: TQ : 095475.

An interesting all weather walk with much wild life and good views. A trifle hilly, it includes an attractive section of the N Downs Way, defended by numerous pill boxes against those of Hitler's invading army expected to advance on London in walking boots rather than jack boots. The route passes The Compasses at Gomshall (Walk 15) and the two walks may be combined to make a longer ramble.

1. Turn R out of the pub along the A25 and take the signed bridleway on the L opposite the Grade 1 listed Hunters' Moon Farmhouse. Cross a bridge over the R.Tillingbourne and with a gate ahead take the bridle path nearest to it. Pass houses and at a 'T' junction turn R on a track. Gomshall Marsh is down to the R and there are often 30 or more moorhens and Canada geese foraging in the field. Just past Twiga Lodge on the L turn L on a signed bridleway. At a road turn R under the railway arch, then R again past the charming Malthouse Cottages. Recross the river over the pack-horse bridge at Gomshall Mill and turn L past The Compasses, then R into Colekitchen Lane.

2. In 150 yards turn R on a signed footpath. Cross a farm track via 2 kissing gates and continue in a wooded strip between fields. At a waymarked fence corner on the L fork L and in 80 yards turn R, soon beginning the ascent of the Downs. There is a view L in May of "The Field of The Cloth of Gold," massed buttercups with blue speedwell edging. Also on the L is a nice view of Colekitchen Farm. Go through a small way-marked gate, then turn R between way-marked posts and take the grass path ahead across Hackhurst Down. Go through a gate, then in a few yards a kissing gate on the L. You are now in an enclosure that may contain bighorn sheep. The path sweeps steeply up to the L. Look back for the view, then

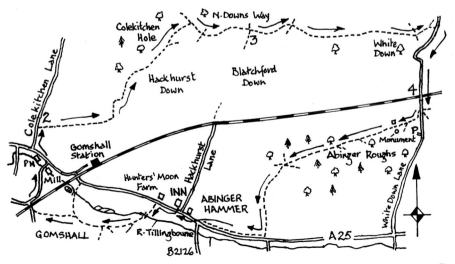

7

Walk No. 1

climb over a turf covered pill box and continue uphill. Reach a fork at the top of a rise and keep ahead L, passing the gaping Colekitchen Hole on your L. Go through a kissing gate and turn R on the N Downs Way. Keep following ND Way signs ignoring all other paths eventually crossing Blatchford Down.

3. Cross the top of Hackhurst Lane via 2 kissing gates at a point common to Walk 15 and maintain direction past 4 more pill boxes. Leave White Down through a gate. In a few yards, at a 4 fingered post, keep ahead passing another pill box on your R, then a large patch of teasels, a favourite feeding place for goldfinches in autumn. At a fingerpost turn R following the ND Way, then turn R on a road for 500yards.

4. Cross the railway bridge and take the first path on the R into Abinger Roughs. At a fork keep ahead R and pass a monument to a fallen cleric on your L. The path is lined with bluebells in season. In summer look out for redstarts, blackcaps and other migrants in these ancient woods. Follow the blue waymarked bridleway ignoring all side paths, eventually uphill with rhododendrons on the R. Cross a grassy clearing with 2 fingerposts and at a waymark post fork L to a farm gate. Continue along the RH edge of the field and out of another gate onto a sunken footpath. Turn R at the A25 onto a footpath above the road and continue past the Abinger Forge back to the pub.

The Abinger Hammer Clock

8

The Jolly Farmer, Bramley.

In a commanding position in the High St opposite the Holy Trinity Church, this superb hostelry has been a village feature for over 200 years and in the same ownership for over 30 years. The comfortable front bar has 2 log fires and a dining extension at the back is in a 350 years old barn rebuilt on the site. The decoration of the barn is remarkable with hops around the cross beams and the walls and ceiling covered in an extraordinary collection of bric à brac, c.f. The Thurlow Arms at Baynards.

The selection of ales from 7 pumps is outstanding and changes regularly. On our visit the full list was Hop Back Summer Lightning, Thunderstorm and Back Row; Hog's Back, TEA and Hair of the Hog; seasonal Spring Ale from Kings of Horsham and Badger Best. There is a choice of 6 wines by the glass.

Bar snacks are sandwiches, jackets and ploughman's in variety, 3 egg omelette and burgers. Main courses include various steaks, cod in beer batter, home cooked smoked ham, chicken with cheddar cheese and chillies and many more. A specials board has fresh fish such as oven baked sea bream, chef's pie of the day, Caribbean mahi mahi and prawns and vegetarian offerings such as roast aubergines and peppers with esquabesh vegetables. On Sundays there is a carvery with a choice of 4 roasts. There is a children's menu and well behaved dogs are welcome in the bar and small patio garden. If you cannot manage to sample all the ales in one sitting, then the 7 en-suite letting rooms and a 3 bedroom flat provide encouragement to stay and fight another day.

Opening hours are Mon-Sat 11am-3pm and 6-11pm; Sun 12-3pm and 7-10.30pm. Tel: 01483 893355.

Walk No. 2

The Jolly Farmer is situated in Bramley High St, part of the A281. There is car parking behind the pub or nearby – see map.

Approx distance of walk 4½ miles. Start at OS Map Ref: TQ009448.

A walk through bluebell woods and over farmland with fine views returning along pretty Thornecombe Street past interesting property and 2 mill ponds.

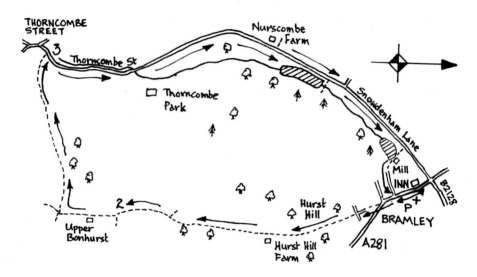

1. Turn R out of the pub along the A281. After Park Drive on the R fork R away from the main road to join a residential road. At a T junction cross to a footpath that leads along the side of Hurst Hill. In spring there are bluebells and in autumn chestnuts to enjoy. You should also see partridges and pheasants unless your visit coincides, as ours did, with one from the alliance of despoilers of the countryside with their guns and dogs. Pass Hurst Hill Farm and later maintain direction past a fingerpost.

2. Join a section of gravel drive to pass Upper Bonhurst. At a T junction turn R, then in a few yards cross a stile on the R into a field. Bear half L up the field to another waymarked stile, remembering to look back

for the view. Enter a copse and follow the path ahead to exit over a stile. Keep to the RH side of 3 fields separated by stiles, then join a track that leads out to Thornecombe Street.

3. Turn R along this quiet lane beside a stream. You pass Thornecombe Park and the Grade 1 listed Nurscombe Farm, then a large mill pond. After passing Iron Lane on the L, signed to Godalming, you may have to contend with a little traffic before reaching another mill pond on the R. Cross the bridge and turn R down the side of the pond, passing Bramley Mill on the L. Continue along Mill Lane and, back at the High St, turn L back to the pub.

The Duke's Head, Brockham.

The Duke's Head is a friendly, comfortable pub nestling on the Greensand Way in the corner of Brockham's famous village green. The central bar has rooms at both ends warmed by gas fires in winter. Exposed beams and bricks and a collection of jugs and tankards hanging from the ceiling create a nice atmosphere and the sun shines through the south facing windows overlooking the green. There are tables outside front and rear. Children are welcome and dogs must be prepared to meet Wilf, an unusually tall Staffordshire bull terrier.

The ales are London Pride and Adnams Bitter and there is a choice of wines by the glass.

The wide ranging menu, all on blackboards, offers a choice of 6 hot baguettes, ploughman's, lasagne and vegetable lasagne, spinach and ricotta filo parcels, steak and ale pie, pork and leek sausages, grilled plaice, salmon and tuna, Cajun chicken salad, curries and chillies and many more.

Opening hours are Mon-Thur 12-3pm and 6-11pm, Fri-Sun open all day from 12 noon. Food is served to 2.30pm daily.

Tel: 01737 841106.

Walk No. 3

Brockham is reached by turning south off the A25 on Brockham Lane, 1½ miles east of Dorking. In ½ mile cross the single track bridge over the R.Mole and take the second turning L along the top of the Brockham village green. The Duke's Head is in the far corner and there is parking behind the pub.

Approx distance of walk 4¾ miles. Start at OS Map Ref: TQ198497.

An easy walk over farmland with fine views and through bluebell woods via the village of Strood Green. In winter there may be mud around Bushbury Farm. The walk may be combined with Walk 4 at the start or at Pondtail Farm.

1, Turn R out of the pub along the lane. This is the Greensand Way. Pass the Royal Oak (Walk 4) and cross Brockham Lane into Old School Lane. Cross the bridge and turn R on the signed cycleway. Just before a pond turn L over a GW waymarked stile. Follow the waymarks over a series of stiles passing the entrance to Pondtail Farm and on over stiles and footbridges keeping the hedge on your R. Pass Bushbury Farm over to the L and maintain direction to reach Tanner's Brook. Walk beside it to a footbridge and stile leading to Tilehurst Lane. Turn L over the road bridge and in 25 yards turn R over a stile onto a track. Just before a green gate fork L and follow the ditch to a waymarked stile by a gate. Maintain direction, now with the ditch on your L, to reach a stile on the L. Cross into a bluebell wood and at an immediate fork keep L. Go over a stile and at a waymark post turn R along a field edge. At the end of the field turn L along the fence and enjoy the view to Brockham and Box Hill.

2. A pinch stile leads to a road, where turn R uphill to a fingerpost on the L. Cross a field to a stile into Highridge Woods. Ignore immediate R and L turns and go ahead on the main path. Go over 2 waymarked crossing paths and at a 'T' junction turn L on a bridleway. At a fork keep L ahead. Go over a wide crossing track and stay on the bridleway ignoring all side paths. Turn R at a 'T' junction soon joining, Tweed Lane, and at the end turn R into Middle Street.

3. Just past the 40mph sign turn L over a stile and along the RH side of 3 fields. In the bottom corner of the third field ignore a stile on the R and turn L beside the hedge. Continue via stiles along 4 fields. The village of Strood Green is visible to the L. At a road turn L then R into Wheelers Lane. Just past Weir Mead Farm turn R at a fingerpost. Cross a stile and bear L to a waymark post in a wire fence. Turn R along the fence. Maintain direction when the fence ends and bear L at a fingerpost passing a bluebell wood on the R to reach a stile. Bear half L down the field to a stile and footbridge and turn R on a fenced path. Back on Wheelers Lane turn R. Just before the church turn R through a barrier and up the RH side of the green back to the pub.

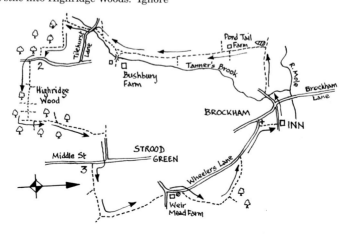

12

The Royal Oak, Brockham.

This deservedly popular, small, friendly pub has a tiny front bar with a log burning stove, 2 tables and a dartboard. Dogs are welcome here. On the other side is the dining area with about 8 tables, where children are welcome if glued to their seats. There are sunny tables outside at the front overlooking picturesque Brockham Green, shady tables at the rear and a grassy playground beyond the car park.

Resident ales are Harvey's Sussex and London Pride with 2 guests, Bombardier and Marstons Bitter on our visit.

There is a good selection of sandwiches, baguettes, jackets and ploughman's. Vegetarians are well catered for with versions of lasagne, burgers, sausage and mash and vegetable kiev. Fresh tuna steak with lime butter and fresh vegetables was superb value in 2004. Main courses also include rump, sirloin and gammon steaks, plaice stuffed with prawns, spicy chicken and avocado salad, chilli and ham, egg and chips and a choice of 4 meals for children.

Opening hours are Mon-Thur 11am-3pm and 5.30-11pm; Fri-Sun open all day from 11am (Sun 12).

Tel: 01737 843241.

Walk No. 4

Brockham is reached by turning south off the A25 on Brockham Lane, 1½ miles east of Dorking. In ¾ mile cross the single track bridge over the R. Mole and take the first or second turning left along the top of Brockham village green. The Royal Oak is on the L. Parking is behind the pub or at the roadside.

Approx distance of walk 5½ miles. Start at OS Map Ref : TQ **197497**.

A walk that commences on the Greensand Way (GW) along the old coach road to Dorking and continues through woods enhanced by bluebells and rhododendrons in season before returning over farmland. There is much bird life and many fine views. The walk may be combined with Walk 3 at the start or at Pondtail Farm.

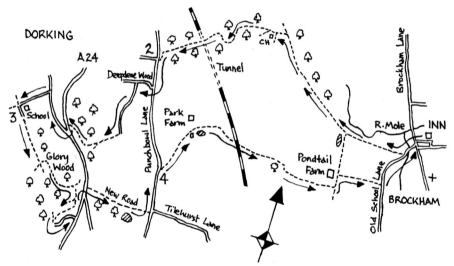

1. Turn R out of the pub and cross Brockham Lane into Old School Lane. Cross the bridge over Tanner's Brook and fork R on the old coach road, now a signed cycle-way. This excellent walk for birdwatchers began well here with parakeets, yellow hammers, long tailed tits, redwings and siskins all in evidence. Pass a pond and metal gates and go over 2 golf course crossing paths. There are nice views to the R. After a metal gate cross the Golf Club drive to a fingerpost and take the first footpath on the L uphill. Opposite the Club House fork R into woods. The A25 roars below and on the R there are views up the Mole Valley to Norbury Park House. At a fork at the end of the fence on the R keep ahead. Go over a crossing path, pass a waymark post and join a tarmac drive downhill to reach Punchbowl Lane opposite Ladygate Rd.

2. Turn L uphill and take the first turning on the R, Deepdene Wood, a residential road. At a waymarked junction by a post box turn L, still uphill. Continue to the end of the road and by Deepdene End turn R, way-marked GW, passing a seat with a fine view. At a waymark post fork R down steps through rhododendrons, pass a Deepdene Terraces notice board and descend to the A24. Turn L briefly, then cross at the central reservation and turn R into Chart Lane. Take the first turning L, St Paul's Rd East.

3. Go through a kissing gate at the top and turn L past the school at a fingerpost signed Glory Wood. Go through a gate and uphill with woods to your L. Go through a gate into Glory Wood and turn L following the orange arrow. At a fork keep L past a GW waymark. A viewpoint on the L gives another sighting of Norbury Park House and Box Hill. At the next waymarked fork go R downhill through bluebells. Pass a waymark on your R, join a garden fence on your L, keep L at 2 forks and exit Glory Wood onto a residential road, Glenwood. Follow this road down to the A24. Cross carefully and turn

L. Pass Chart Lane South and take the next track on the R before the Dorking Golf Club sign. Go through the Golf Club overflow car park, then over 2 crossing paths and on when the track becomes a path to emerge on Knowle Lane. Turn L uphill.

4. Where the road bends R fork R on a signed footpath. There are fine views of Park Farm and beyond. Bluebells to your L and skylarks above may help to lighten your step on the last lap. Just beyond some barns turn R at a fingerpost passing a pond on the

R. Go through a waymarked gate and under a railway arch, then between fields. At fingerposts turn R, then L and over a stile. Follow the GW arrow along the LH side of 2 fields. Cross a stile and a footbridge. Turning R here would join Walk 3, but for this walk turn L to the gate to Pondtail Farm, then turn R on the farm drive. Reach Old School Lane and turn L. Recross Tanner's Brook and continue back to the pub.

Park Farm, Brockham

The Crown, Capel.

Our first visit to The Crown was on St Patrick's Day. The Irish barman had put on a tape of fiddly diddly music and the chorus of one number summed up our morning.

    All God's creatures have a place in the choir
    Some sing low and some sing higher
    Some sing loud from the telegraph wire
    Others just clap their hands

The sun shone and the birds and even a couple of donkeys had given it their best and we just clapped. The handsome Crown free house did nothing to dispel our euphoria with Singing Postman and High Speed Train from the Somerset Cottage microbrewery, Hogs Back TEA and local Horsham Best and a good choice of wines. Dating from the mid 17th century the Grade II listed Crown reveals its age with a Horsham slab roof, exposed timbers and an interesting central chimney with back to back fireplaces warming the lounge and public bars. On the front of the building is a rare South American trumpet vine and there is a restaurant extension at the rear.

Justly renowned for its food, the extensive blackboard menu includes jackets, burgers, hot and cold baguettes, ploughman's, a good salad selection and freshly made pizzas. There are steaks, mixed grill, calves liver and bacon, butterfly chicken and a range of pasta and vegetarian dishes, while a specials board has further delights. The pizzas, fish and chips, scampi, curry and chilli are all available to take away.

Children have their own menu and a play area in the garden, where an impressive looking barbecue was under construction in April 2004. Dogs welcome inside and out.

Opening hours are Mon-Fri 12-3pm and 4.30-11.30pm; weekends open all day from 11am Sat and 12 Sun.

Tel: 01306 711130.

Capel is signed from the A24 at Beare Green and the A29 at Ockley. The pub is in the centre of the village next to the church and there is parking there. The walk passes close to Ockley Station and can be joined from there – see map. The station is a little over a mile from The Inn on The Green at Ockley (Walk 29) should you wish to combine the walks.

Approx distance of walk 4¼ miles. Start at OS Map Ref : TQ 175407.

A lovely walk best done at bluebell time as they are everywhere in the woods. Birdsong is another bonus in the spring and a local reported a short eared owl hunting over the rough meadows in section 2. Mud will be a problem in the winter.

1. Turn L out of the pub and L through the lych gate of St John the Baptist church. Continue through the churchyard to a kissing gate in the back fence. Continue along a field and cross the waymarked RH stile. Maintain direction over more fields and stiles. After the 4th stile turn L on a farm track for 15 yards then R over a stile and bear half L to a stile in the bottom corner of the field. Bear L across waste ground to a stile leading to the grass verge of the A24. Turn L then L again into Cole's Lane. Just past Bennett's Wood on the L turn R on a signed path. (This little bluebell wood is criss crossed with paths. I have described one route through but if you get lost keep bearing L away from the A24 back to Cole's Lane.) At a fork keep L and at a crossing path before a stile turn L, then immediately fork R. Keep on the widest path to cross a ditch and bear R to a path junction where you take the third exit ahead. At the next junction take the central path of 3 ahead. At the next fork go L, then fork L through holly bushes. Finally fork R over a hump and steeply down to a small car park in Cole's Lane. Turn R then R again into Horsham Rd. In 40 yards turn L on a signed path. Pass a kissing gate and fork L. Fork R before a gate, join a fence on the L and go up a slope passing a gate on the L.

2. Pause at the top and look back for a fine view over Capel. Turn R through the kissing gate and in a few yards fork L on a grass path beside bushes on the L. Ignore a sleeper bridge on the L and continue over a sleeper bridge and stile, then bear L along the field edge. At a 3 fingered post bear R following the arrow across a large field to a fingerpost on the edge of a bluebell wood. Turn L along the field edge and in the corner turn L again beside another bluebell wood. Ignore a waymarked stile and at a 3 fingered post by a gate turn R on a wide track through the wood. Ignore side paths, pass a house on the L and at a road turn R.

3. Turn L into the drive to Temple Mead. Before the main gates go through a gate on the R, then keep L on the grass beside a hedge. Exit through another gate and turn L to a stile and continue between fences and along the LH side of a field. Cross 2 stiles into a bluebell wood, this one also blessed with a few primroses. Maintain direction over a sleeper bridge and stile and across a field to a railed footbridge over Mizbrook. There were deer among the bluebells here. Go forward to a crossing track and turn L, where there is a good display of foxgloves in season. In 10 yards turn R and fork L immediately to a stile. Go up the RH side of the field noting the view R at the top. Just before a waymarked stile turn L down the field edge to a stile into a copse. Cross a sleeper bridge and turn L at a T junction. Follow the path bending R through a clearing, over a crossing track and under power lines. Go down to a sleeper bridge and stile and then along the LH side of a field. Cross a stile on the L and turn R along the hedge to a stile by a gate, then on through Mizbrook Farm to a road.

4. Turn L for 100 yards, then turn R at a fingerpost into Mizbrook Yard. Go through a barrier on the L before a gate and follow a fenced drive. Cross a footbridge on the R and go along a fence into a recreation ground. Turn L along the LH edge to a footbridge in the corner. Turn L on a path and at a road turn R back to the pub.

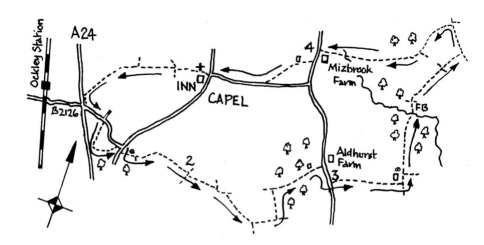

St John the Baptist, Capel

The Rising Sun, Charlwood.

We caught the century old Rising Sun behind a cloud by visiting on the Tuesday after a bumper May Bank Holiday. They had sold most of their food and ale and were desperately awaiting replenishment by tardy suppliers. The menu usually offers good basic pub grub including a nice choice of sandwiches and baguettes, plain and toasted, jackets, omelettes and ploughman's. Main courses include sirloin and gammon steaks, beer battered cod and haddock (to take away Fridays and Saturdays), scampi, all day breakfast and vegetarian breakfast, Cumberland sausage and vegetarian specials like Quorn fillets with pepper sauce.

The ales are London Pride and Greene King IPA.

Stretching back from the front bar there is a room with a couple of settees leading to a restaurant extension and a rear garden, barbecue and patio. Enjoying our ploughman's in the sunshine we were surprised by a flurry of sparrows diving for cover in an elderberry bush. Looking up a kestrel was hovering directly overhead but my offer of a pickled onion was spurned.

Children and dogs are welcome.

Opening hours are Mon-Sat: 11am-11pm and Sun 12-10.30pm. Lunchtime food is served from 12-2.30pm.

Tel: 01293 863709.

Walk No. 6

Charlwood is reached from the A25 east of Dorking via Brockham and Leigh or from the A217 and A24 north of Gatwick Airport via Hookwood. The Rising Sun is on the main road in the centre of the village and has its own car park.

Approx distance of walk 4½ miles. Start at OS Map Ref : TQ 243411.

A walk that starts on the Sussex Border Path, passes interesting old property and crosses farmland to two bluebell woods before ending past an ancient church with mediaeval wall paintings. The walk passes within ½ mile of The Fox Revived (Walk 28 – see para 3) should you wish to enjoy a longer ramble.

1. Turn L out of the pub passing the village green and turn L into Chapel Rd. You are now on the Sussex Border Path. After Swan Lane on the L continue on a track past Providence Chapel, reminiscent in name and appearance of a settlers' chapel in nineteenth century America. At a 4 fingered post turn L on a Byway into sheep country. This is Pudding Lane and in spring the fields on both sides are full of lambs and yellowhammers sing from the hedge tops. Go through a gate and at a road turn L. After about 300 yards turn R into Rectory Lane passing the Grade 1 listed Lavender Cottage. After Barkers Cottages turn R on an unsigned drive that passes the 17th century former school house, now Bristow's Cottage, with its Horsham slab roof. Cross a stile by a gate and follow the RH field margin over 3 more stiles, through a small copse and on to a final stile.

2. At a road by Barfield Farm bear L on a signed footpath beside the road. Pass the end of Beggarshouse Lane and stay on the grass verge for 100 yards, then cross the road into the Woodland Trust's Edolphs Copse. You can wander at will in this lovely bluebell wood and nature reserve but, for the purposes of this walk, go forward for 15 yards then turn L. At an information board turn R, then L at a waymark post. At a fork go R following the white arrow post. Cross a sleeper bridge by a pond and turn R at the waymark post. Fork R, then L still following white arrows and pass an enclosure on your L. At a crossing track with a sleeper bridge on your R turn L and at a fork go R. Take the second R turn to reach a gate, where turn R on the road.

3. At the road junction The Fox Revived (Walk 28) is ¾ mile along Norwood Hill if you want to extend the walk. Otherwise

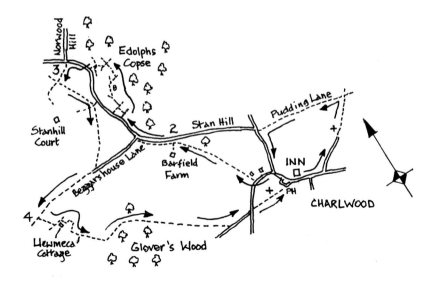

turn L into an entrance drive signed to Stanhill Court Hotel. Look for a stile on the L and follow the waymark across a field to a stile in a wire fence, then on to a kissing gate in the hedge below. Cross the statue lined main hotel drive and go through another kissing gate. Head across another large field passing to the L of an island copse and on to a waymarked stile in the RH hedge. Go between 2 fence posts and cross a small field diagonally to a stile. Turn R on Beggarshouse Lane, that soon narrows to a footpath. Continue for ¼ mile to a stile on the L.
4. Cross the field passing to the L of a line of oak trees to a stile behind the last tree. Turn L on a farm track, then R past Llewmeca Cottage. Follow the waymarked fence around 3 sides of the cottage grounds, then turn L along the field edge with a hedge on your R. Ignore a stile on the R and cross a stile at the bottom into Glover's Wood, another bluebell wood and nature reserve. At a fork go L, ignore a R turn and continue to a stile into a field. Turn R along the hedge to a stile and through a copse into another large field. Cross this diagonally to a stile in the bottom LH corner. Follow the path to a stile by Brookside and turn L on a road. Cross Rectory Lane to a footpath that leads into St Nicholas' churchyard. The 900 years old church is usually open and the medieval wall painting and carved screen should not be missed. Leave the churchyard and pass the Half Moon on your R and continue down the road back to the Rising Sun.

Providence Chapel, Charlwood

St Nicholas, Charlwood

The Winterton Arms, Chiddingfold.

The original part of The Winterton Arms is 300 years old. It was called The Gateway because it was adjacent to a toll point on the road but subsequently renamed in honour of the Earl of Winterton, MP. It is a jolly pub, a bit noisy and 'blokey' at weekends but one noise is not welcome – if your mobile phone rings in the pub it will be consigned to the fish tank! Log fires make you welcome and there is a separate dining room to one side. Children are welcome here and in the pleasant garden equipped with a playground and sometimes a bouncy castle. Dogs are welcome in the bar.

The ales are Ansells Bitter, London Pride and Youngs Special and there is a choice of wines by the glass.

The menu, all on blackboards, has a good range of snacks, baguettes and jackets with homemade burgers and veggy burgers. Top of the main courses is the 'Winterton' fillet steak with prawns, bacon and mushrooms and staples include marinaded lamb steak, cottage pie, steak and kidney pudding, hot asparagus quiche, 10 inch American pizza, chilli, lasagne, fish and chips and vegetarian sausage. N.B No food Sunday evenings. In June 2004 they did not accept credit cards.

Opening hours are: Mon-Fri 11.30am-3pm and 5.30-11pm, Sat 11.30am-11pm and Sun 12-10.30pm.

Tel: 01428 683221.

The Winterton Arms is on the A283 about ½ mile north of Chiddingfold centre. There is ample parking in front of and behind the pub.

Approx distance of walk 5 miles. Start at OS Map Ref : SU 964365.

A walk in woods bursting with birdsong and over farmland much of it beside the R Lox, a tributary of the Arun. There are deer, pheasants, wild garlic, orchids and bluebells in the woods and an immaculate 13th century church and a holy well at Dunsfold. We did this walk comfortably in February but you will need boots for the muddy bridleways.

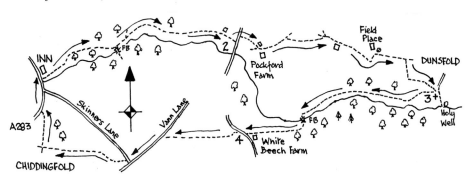

1. Turn L out of the pub and at the end of the car park turn L on a footpath through a yard and between fences into woods beside the R Lox. Pass a footbridge on the R, cross a sleeper bridge and at a fork keep ahead R. We saw 3 kinds of wagtail here pied, grey and yellow. The woods end and at a wooden fence corner go through a gate, then turn L and R through another gate into a field. Continue along the LH side of a meadow. Cross a footbridge and maintain direction across 2 meadows and through gates to pass a house on your L and continue down the drive.

2. Turn L on the road and in 100 yards turn R down the drive to Pockford Farm. In front of the farm turn L past an aviary and continue on a farm track. Where this bends R go ahead through a waymarked gate and up the LH side of a field to a 4 fingered post. Turn R and follow the faint path across the field to a sleeper bridge, then along the LH side of the next field. There are nice views of Hydons Ball and Hascombe Hill to the L. Pass a waymarked gate on the L, then fork L and through a gate. Turn L in front of a barn and down the long farm drive. The drive bends L towards Field Place, then R past a pond. Just past 2 five bar gates on opposite sides cross a stile on the R and go down the RH side of the field, then turn L

along the bottom to a stile in the corner. Bear half R across a small field and over a stile into a churchyard. St Mary and All Saints, Dunsfold dates from around 1280 and still has some original locally made pews and the remnants of an ancient yew tree. Swifts nest above the porch. If you go out of the lych gate and turn R down the track you come to a holy well. The water here is supposed to be beneficial for eye complaints but be sure to boil it first!

3. Retrace your steps to cross the stile by which you entered the churchyard. Turn L along the hedge, through a gate, then another into woods with a field on the L. Go through a waymarked gate and turn L, then immediately R along the RH side of a field. Pass a waymark and continue beside the river to a gate. Cross a footbridge and keep beside the river through woods carpeted with wild garlic. Go through a small waymarked gate, cross a railed footbridge and go uphill into woods past a badger set. At a field corner continue with a fence on your L to the gate to White Beech Farm.

4. Turn R on the road for 100 yards, then L on a signed wide grass bridleway. This narrows between fields and there is a glorious patch of early purple orchids on the R in early May. At a road, Vann Lane, turn L for ¼ mile, then take the first R turn, Skinners

Walk No. 7

Lane, signed to Witley. In 25 yards turn L at a fingerpost onto a footpath. Fork R at a waymark, now with a hedge on the L. A flock of 50 greenfinches watched our passing from the telegraph wires. Go through a waymarked field gap and turn R, now with the hedge on your R. At he end of the field turn R at a waymark and, in a few yards, fork R before a gate and across a field. Maintain direction over 3 stiles, then bear L to the A283 and turn R back to the pub.

St Mary and All Saints, Dunsfold

Early Purple Orchids

The Plough, Coldharbour.

This 17th century hostelry and brewery has long been one of my favourite pubs and real ale drinkers are assured of satisfaction in the bar of the Plough free house.

The ales change regularly but expect to see 3 or 4 from Tanglefoot, Spitfire, Timothy Taylor's The Landlord, Ringwood Old Thumper, Sussex bitter and the like. They will in any case be supplemented by landlord Rick Abrehart's own Leith Hill Brewery offerings such as Crooked Furrow and Tallywhacker.

There is an attractive restaurant and 2 small bars linked by a central fire. When the pub overflows with walkers there is an overspill barn with wooden tables and an open fire in winter. If you become captivated by the pub and the excellent walking hereabouts there are 7 en suite letting rooms.

The bar menu has a choice of 6 ploughman's, baguettes, soup of the day with a crusty roll, chicken Caesar and tomato mozzarella and red onion salads, 2 vegetarian meals, e.g. wild mushroom Stroganoff with rice, 4 or 8oz rib eye steaks, pork and leek sausage and mash, etc. Homemade puddings are a speciality. There is a children's menu and dogs on leads are welcome in the bars.

Hours are Mon-Fri 11am-3pm and 6-11pm; weekends open all day.

Tel: 01306 711793.

Walk No. 8

The Plough is in the centre of Coldharbour and can be reached by turning south off the A25 on Coldharbour Lane in Dorking or Hollow Lane in Wotton. Alternatively, from the A29 turn north on Broomehall Rd 1 mile north of Ockley. The walk may be joined from Holmwood Railway Station – see map. There is limited car parking outside the pub but there are 2 car parks on the Abinger Rd to the west.

Approx distance of walk 4 miles. Start at OS Map Ref : TQ 152441.

The most popular walk from The Plough is up Leith Hill – see Walk No. 15 in "Forty Walks in S. Surrey" but this is a pleasant venture into the foothills through fields and several bluebell woods with fine views in places.

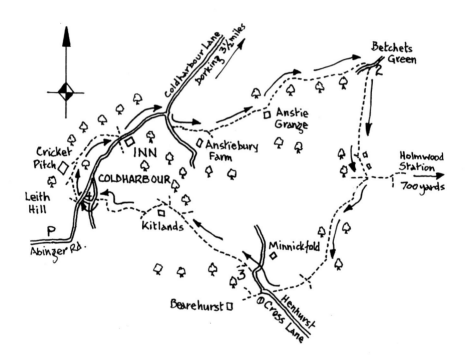

1. Turn R out of the pub up the road and at a 'T' junction turn R. Up to your R is the iron age hill fort of Anstiebury. At the entrance to a concrete drive on the L cross a stile and turn R along the fence to another stile, where cross back and continue on the drive. Strange waymarking to muse upon as you maintain direction between farm buildings with Anstiebury Farmhouse over to the R. Pass a stile on the R and continue between fields. Cross a waymarked stile, then another beside the gate to Taresmocks and on down hill into a bluebell wood. The wood narrows to a strip, then after a foot-

bridge widens again. Cross a stile and keep to the RH side of a field to a stile onto a road.
2. Cross the road and bear R to a stile into the National Trust owned Betchets Brook Fields. Keep beside the fence on the R up 3 fields connected by stiles, the last of which leads into a copse. The bluebells here are sprinkled with wood anemones. Join a track and keep ahead passing gardens on the L. At a track junction turn R on the signed footpath. (Left here is the way to Holmwood Railway Station). At a fork go R through a gate onto a tarmac drive. There are more bluebells and wood anemones and you cross

a burbling stream. At a fingerpost fork R on the tarmac passing the rather grand Minnickfold on the R. Turn R along Henhurst Cross Lane but as you do so sneak a peek through the leylandii ahead at the pretty pond and resident geese in the grounds of Bearehurst opposite.

3. After 150 yards turn L at a fingerpost into yet another bluebell wood. At a fork go R to cross a stile just past a gate. Turn L along the field edge and maintain direction to reach a stile and footbridge on the L. Cross and bear R diagonally up the field with lovely views all round to a stile to the R of a wooden stable block. Turn L on a lane past Kitlands Cottages, ignoring a fingerpost on the R. At a fork keep L downhill and

at a fingerpost turn R on the footpath. Go through a gate and bear L at a waymark post uphill. Keep following waymarks to a small gate, where turn R between fences, then turn R on a drive. Opposite Chasemore Cottage turn L up to a road and turn L again up to Christ Church. From the church gate fork L past The Old Vicarage and at a 'T' junction turn L. In 150 yards at a NT notice take the path on the R up wooden steps and along the hillside. At a waymark post turn R on a wider path. (Left here would take you up Leith Hill). There is a fine view south on the R and on the L you pass the highest cricket pitch in Surrey. Join a wide sandy track and follow this downhill back to the pub.

Christ Church, Coldharbour

27

The Pilgrim, Dorking.

The pub is about 150 years old and was the Station Tavern before being renamed for the Pilgrims' Way. It still has some railway memorabilia on show, along with enough references to the Titanic to give you that sinking feeling. Not for long though, as this bustling friendly establishment has a real pub atmosphere to lift the spirits. There is a dining area one side of the bar and a pool table on the public bar side, where dogs are welcome.

The ales are Ringwoods Best and Old Thumper, London Pride and Adnams Bitter.

A good selection of sandwiches and baguettes is available with a choice of 6 ploughman's, 6 jackets, 4 salads, pizzas and bowls of mussels. Main courses include various steaks, chicken fajitas, excellent cod in beer batter, lasagne etc. A specials board had shoulder of lamb, steak and ale pie and fresh fillet of plaice in beer batter or in prawn and lobster sauce. The 'fillet' turned out to be 5 small fillets piled up in a cheffy tower. Excellent food, nicely presented, prompt service and value for money. In such circumstances it seems churlish to mention that there is a 10% service charge for groups of 10 or more. Ramblers Association parties may wish to form up in nines before entering and ignore one another until clear of the premises? The landlord would be grateful for prior notice of large groups – you can ring ahead and place your orders. Food service ends at 2pm. Children are admitted only when dining but there is an attractive garden.

Opening hours are Mon-Fri 11am-3pm and 5.30-11pm. Weekends open all day. This is a good centre for walks in the Box Hill area and there are 5 rooms available for bed and breakfast.

Tel: 01306 889951.

The Pilgrim is on the approach to Dorking West Station. From the A25 in central Dorking turn north on the A2003 Station Rd and fork L and L again towards the station. Alternatively from the A24 turn W on the A2003, Ashcombe Rd, for ¾ mile, continue L when this becomes Chalkpit Lane and turn sharp R into Station Rd, then fork L.

Approx distance of walk 5 miles. Start at OS Map Ref : TQ 161498.

A walk up the slopes of a vineyard and across Ranmore Common, through Dorking Wood and back along the N Downs Way and Pilgrims' Way. There are superb views in places and bluebells in season. The walk may be combined with either Walk 16 or Walk 38, both of which pass through point 2.

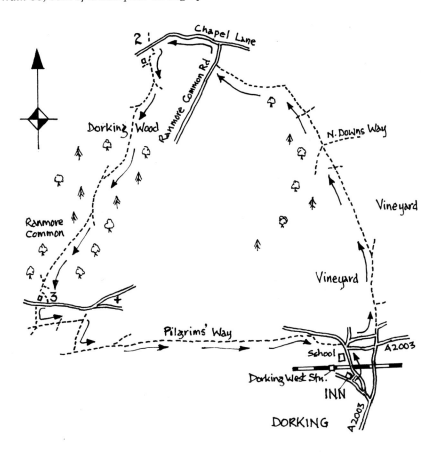

1. Turn L out of the pub and immediately L again through the car park and on to a 'T' junction, where turn L. Cross the railway and pass a school. Turn R into Limeway Terrace, then R again into Chalkpit Terrace. Ignore a L turn and at the end of the road turn L. At a fork go L, signed Westhumble 1 mile and at the next fingerpost fork L, soon downhill through the vineyard. Go through a kissing gate and continue on a wide track to another fingerpost, where fork L on a grass path. There are views to Box Hill on the R and Norbury Park ahead. At a fingerpost just past a pylon keep ahead on a

grass path. Cross a stile to a 4 fingered post, where cross the N Downs Way and maintain direction into woods carpeted with wood anemones and bluebells in season. Continue on a fenced track and then on the tarmac drive of Ashleigh Grange, passing a fine redwood tree. Before the drive bends R fork L with the fence to a stile. Follow the yellow waymark up the field keeping just to the left of the power lines to a stile by a gate. Bear L on a fenced path down hill, past a barrier and along a field edge to a stile. Turn R on Ranmore Common Rd and at a 'T' junction turn L on Chapel Lane for ¼ mile.

2. Forty yards past the entrance to Old Dean turn L on a signed bridleway, passing a NT sign for Polesden Lacey. This section to the fork is common to walk 16. At a fork go L between fields and reach 2 gates on the R. Go through the small one and maintain direction up a field past a lone oak to another gate into Dorking Wood. At a fork go L between gate posts. After about ½ mile continue on a track that comes in from the R and soon fork R at a waymark post. Go gen-

tly uphill for another 700 yards and continue past a cluster of bluebells and waymarks to turn L before a garden.

3. At Ranmore Common Rd again turn R for 50 yards, then L to a footpath fingerpost. Pass a waymarked gate and in a few yards turn L onto the N Downs Way and through a gate into Steers Field. Fork R before the sign and enjoy the views. Ranmore Church is ahead L. At a 3 fingered post turn R downhill signed Link to Greensand Way. Go through a kissing gate and discover why I wrote this walk anti-clockwise. At the bottom of this slope turn L on a wide track. This is the Pilgrims' Way although there are no signs to say so and you follow it gently downhill for almost a mile. There are views over Dorking and skylarks above. At a fork go R and at the end of the track at a yellow arrow waymark fork R on a footpath through a copse and on beside a road. Emerge opposite Limeway Crescent and turn R over the railway bridge and retrace your steps back to the pub.

St. Barnabus, Ranmore Common

The Queen's Head, East Clandon.

The pub is a timber framed grade II listed building dating from the 17th century. It was first recorded as a pub, then brewing its own ale, in 1855. Documents in 1888 detail, in addition to the main house, "Brewery, Slaughter House, Butcher's Shop, Club House, Granary Barn, Cart House, Stables for 8 horses, cow shed, piggeries and a large fruit and vegetable garden. Such a significant village institution deserved better from Guildford planners than to allow in the late 1990's a fatuous change of name to The Wishing Well. Fortunately new owners with a better sense of history restored the old name in 2004 but selected Queen Victoria to replace Elizabeth I on the inn sign. The attractive beamed interior is divided into 4 rooms around a central bar and boasts 3 fireplaces, one an inglenook.

The menu includes a good choice of baguettes, jackets and ploughman's, mixed tapas, brie and courgette crumble, various steaks, home-made dishes such as soup of the day, fisherman's pie, chicken curry, steak and kidney pie, fresh cod and haddock and various nicely presented salads, pork and Barnsley chops, steak and kidney, shepherd's and Guinness pies, whole grilled plaice and sea bass and moussaka and vegetarian quiche

The ales are Hogs Back TEA, Harveys Sussex and Old Speckled Hen and there is a choice of wines. Children are welcome, dogs in the small side garden only.

The pub is open Tues-Sat from 11.30am-3pm and 6-11pm, Sun 12-3pm and 6-10.30pm. NB closed all day Mondays and no boots in the pub please.

Tel: 01483 222332.

31

Walk No. 10

East Clandon is reached by a signed turning off the A246 4 miles east of Guildford centre. Cross the Old Epsom Road and the pub is ahead. There is a large car park.

Approx distance of walk 4¾ miles. Start at OS Map Ref : TQ 059517.

The walk may be combined with Walk 27 at Point 3.
A walk commencing in the village of East Clandon with its Norman church and pretty cottages and an optional extension into the National Trust's Hatchlands Park. After skirting a golf course the walk visits another Norman church in West Clandon, then takes a gentle path up Clandon Down to an old racecourse where deer abound. The return, with fine views, crosses farmland where skylarks sing. A short section near the start may be very wet in winter when boots will be essential.

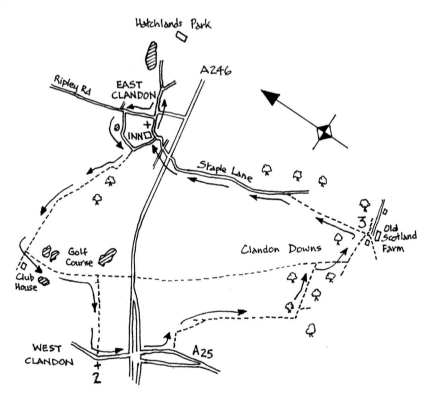

1. Turn L out of the pub passing the 12th century Church of St Thomas of Canterbury, a name with obvious links to the pilgrims' routes across the North Downs. Continue past attractive old cottages and Ripley Road and follow the NT waymark up to the gate of Hatchlands Park. Walks in the grounds, where there is a fine bluebell wood, are an optional extra in summer but are closed from November to April. The house, with interior by Robert Adam, has collections of furniture and musical instruments. Tel : 01483 222482 for opening times. Sheepwash Pond near the gate is a magnet for birds in winter and a cormorant was drying its wings atop the tallest tree on our visit. Retrace your steps to Ripley Rd and turn R, then L into Back Lane. Fork L past the duck pond and turn R past Orchard Cottage onto a signed footpath between hedges. The first

Reporting for Ablutions, Sheepwash Pond in Hatchlands Park

150 yards may be very wet in winter but persevere and you may surprise some of the hundreds of pheasants that often shelter here from flying golf balls. Pass a metal kissing gate and continue along the edge of the golf course to a finger post. Turn L for 25 yards to another finger post, where turn R on the grass. Walk on the ridge of hillocks to another fingerpost and follow that pointer across a fairway to another fingerpost. Cross a footbridge and turn L to join the Golf Club drive for ¼ mile. At a fingerpost cross a footbridge on the R and go ahead on a footpath.
2. Reach a road opposite the church of St Peter and St Paul, West Clandon. The Church was rebuilt in 1760 after partial collapse but still retains a few mediaeval features e.g. a fragment of rood screen and carved piscinas. Turn L past the church and at the traffic lights go ahead over the A246 and along the A25. In 200 yards turn L on a signed footpath between hedges. At a fingerpost bear half R across a field to a fingerpost in a hedge. Turn R between hedges

uphill. At the next fingerpost turn L onto a grass area between hawthorn trees. This is the top of Clandon Down and a local told us that major horse race meetings were held here in the 18th and early 19th centuries. The grassy course widens and there are numerous rabbits and a few deer may shy away before you reach a fence, where turn R along the woodland edge. At a 'T' junction turn L on a signed bridleway. This section as far as Old Scotland Farm is common to Walk 27.
3. With Old Scotland Farm to your R fork L to a stile (Point 4 on Walk 27) and enter woods. Emerge from the woods and walk forward passing a group of 4 trees on your R. Maintain direction down a long field for about 500 yds to a fingerpost and stile in the RH hedge. Turn L into Staple Lane. Surprisingly in January 2004 4 skylarks were singing over the fields on both sides of the lane. Cross the A246 again and go ahead across the Old Epsom Road and back to the pub.

The Prince of Wales, West End, Esher.

The pub dates from the mid 19th century when it was purpose built as part of a combined malt house, brewery and inn. At the time West End was described as a "mostly marshy, stinking and choleraic locality." A far cry from today when the lovely village green sports 2 attractive ponds, home to a variety of water birds. Now part of the Chef and Brewer chain, the pub features a tastefully rendered olde worldiness with ancient timbers, exposed brickwork and collections of plates and pots.

There is a printed snack menu offering jackets, ploughman's, sandwiches, "hot hob" baguettes and salad bowls, e.g. prawn and avocado or Greek and shell on prawns by the pint or ½ pint. The main courses are on blackboards and include fish and chips, steak and kidney pudding, lemon chicken, Thai red chicken curry, roast duck, gammon or pepper steak, noisettes of lamb, etc. Fresh fish is a speciality e.g. grilled whole plaice on the bone or butterfly rainbow trout.

The ales are London Pride, Theakstons's Best and Old Speckled Hen and a guest, e.g. Hogshead Bitter. The selection of 20 wines are all available by the glass. Children are welcome and dogs in the large pleasant garden.

Opening hours are Mon-Sat 11am-11pm, Sun 12-10.30pm. NB. Although large the pub gets very busy at weekends and does not accept bookings.

Tel: 01372 465483.

The West End of Esher is really a separate village. It can be reached by going west from Esher on the A244, Lammas Lane and turning L at the first roundabout into West End Lane. The Prince of Wales is on the R on the corner of Winterdown Rd. From the A3 turn E on the A245 signed Cobham, then E again on the A307 signed Esher for 2½ miles and turn L into West End Lane for ½ mile. There is parking at the pub.

Approx distance of walk 4½ miles. Start at OS Map Ref : TQ 129639.

A lovely walk mostly in woods and beside the R. Mole. There are bluebells in season and pretty ponds with birds and dragonflies. The commons are criss crossed with paths so close attention to route finding is necessary.

1. Turn R out of the pub down Winterdown Rd or on the grass verge beside the pond. In 2004 the 7 species of water birds on the pond included a ruddy shelduck. Keep beside the road to reach a fingerpost opposite Garson Farm, where turn L signed to Esher Common 1 mile. Pass strawberry fields on the R, keep ahead where the bridleway forks L and at a fork at the end of the fields go R to a waymark post. A few yards on gives a fine view over the R. Mole and beyond. Return to the post and turn R down steps, then L along the riverbank. Boardwalks assist your progress over boggy areas where kingcups thrive and bluebells are interspersed with rhododendrons and patches of wild garlic. Pass under power lines and past a seat to reach a fingerpost.

2. Turn L uphill helped by steps. Just past a barrier turn L and at a fork go R, then over a crossing path and through an avenue of rhododendrons. Pass a white house and turn sharp R at a crossing path down to the A307. Cross over past a bridleway waymark and at a crossing track turn L. In a few yards fork R, then fork L past a horse barrier and along a shady avenue. After the next barrier turn R, keep R at an immediate fork and you are soon beside Black Pond. Continue past the end of the pond and at a fingerpost turn L signed Oxshott Heath. As you approach a footbridge over the A3 look for a bridleway waymark on the R and fork L into woods. The path bends R and then forks R to a barrier, where turn L on a wide track over a bridge and gently uphill to

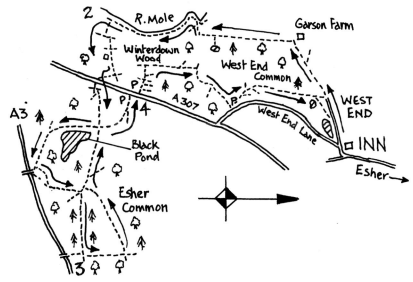

the 'Five Ways' path junction. Take the second path on the R signed Arbrook Common ¾ m.

3. With the A3 at a crescendo again turn L on a wide crossing track, where a fingerpost tells you that Arbrook Common is still ½ m. Go uphill and down to a fingerpost and turn L signed Fairmile Common ¾ m. Keep L at a waymarked fork and ignore side paths to reach the Five Ways Junction again. Turn R, signed Winterdown Wood, then fork L signed Portsmouth Rd ¾ m. At a fork keep R and at a barrier turn R on the crossing track from Black Pond. Pass 2 information boards and go over a crossing path to reach the A307.

4. Cross over and turn R up to a car park. Cross the car park to a notice board and take the path behind it. Ignore both the immedi-

ate R fork and a second R fork. Go over a crossing path and at the next fork by a tree stump carved into a dolphin shape go L. Pass a barrier and turn R on a wide bridleway, soon downhill. At a fork at the bottom of the hill keep R ahead to reach a seat, where turn R on a wide track. Go over a hump past the remains of a brick wall and turn L. Pass another seat and turn L on a crossing path through a clearing. At a fork keep R. Just before a car park turn sharp L on a grass path and at a fork keep L. At the next fork keep R and fork L before a seat. Go through a barrier and follow a fingerpost signed West End Village. This raised path takes you through the marshy area that may have given rise to the 19th century stink. Pass a small pond and cross the village green back to the pub.

Church of St. Peter and St. Paul, Ewhurst, Walk No. 12

The Bull's Head, Ewhurst.

The large and comfortable Bull's Head was built as a railway hotel before the belated decision was taken not to extend the line to Ewhurst. Even if the line had opened Beeching would have closed it long ago anyway. Now owned by Pubmaster and nicely decorated with farming and forestry implements, the pub is very popular with walkers. It has a large nicely maintained beer garden with a patio and a separate well equipped play area.

The ales are Flowers IPA, Pedigree and Adnams Bitter and there is a choice of 8 wines by the glass.

The extensive menu, all on blackboards, includes sandwiches, jackets, ploughman's and a choice of 8 salads. Vegetarians are catered for with moussaka and lasagne. Homemade steak and kidney pie, chicken curry, ham egg and chips, half a duck a l'orange and grilled swordfish are all regulars and the specials board features the likes of boiled beef and dumplings, chicken Provencale, prawn and mango salad and sautéed lambs kidneys. "Senior citizen" and children's meals are also available. Dogs are welcome in the garden only.

Opening hours are Mon-Sat 11am-2.30pm and 6-11pm; Sun 12-2.30pm and 6-10.30pm.

Tel: 01483 277447.

Walk No. 12

Ewhurst is on the B2127 mid way between Forest Green and Cranleigh. The Bull's Head is at the northern end of the village at the junction of the B2127 and Shere Rd.

Approx distance of walk 4¾ miles. Start at OS Map Ref : TQ 090409.

A walk through extensive bluebell woods and across farmland with a good chance of seeing deer. Bridleways can be very muddy in winter.

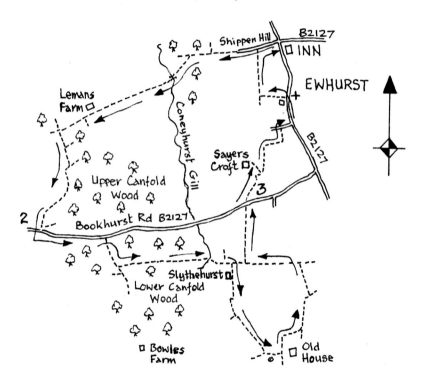

1. Go forward across the road from the front of the pub past a weeping willow tree into Shippen Hill. There are wood anemones in the grass verge to the R and bluebells in the woods beyond. The road narrows and enters woods. After 150 yards take the path on the L at a fingerpost. Cross a footbridge over Coneyhurst Gill and bear half R to a stile into a field. Follow a fingerpost direction down the edge of a long field with a nice view to the R. Cross a stile and go between fences. Maintain direction over 4 more stiles, cross over the track leading into Lemans Farm and continue on a bridleway into a bluebell wood. Follow this sometimes muddy path downhill to a finger post, where turn L on a crossing bridleway.

Ignore paths on the L and keep on to reach the B2127, Cranleigh Rd.
2. Cross over and turn L on the pavement up Bookhurst Hill. The heavy clay on your boots from the woods is put to better use here by the tile manufacturer, formerly Bookhurst Pottery. Continue on the grass verge when the pavement ends and turn R at a fingerpost onto the drive to Bowles Farm. After 150 yards turn L over a way-marked sleeper bridge into Lower Canfield Wood. At a 'T' junction turn L, then R before a barrier and over a crossing track. Briefly join a fence to reach a stile, then continue along the RH side of a field. Cross a farm track via 2 stiles and continue with a fence on the R. Cross a footbridge and a stile

to turn L on a drive. At a 'T' junction bear half R to a stile, Go along the RH fence for 25 yards and turn R over a stile, cross a track and go between hedges past the lovely Slythehurst farmhouse. Leave the garden via a stile and a sleeper bridge and continue beside a low electric fence. Where this ends at a wooden fence step over it carefully to the R and at the corner turn L along the hedge to a gate. Cross the next 2 fields diagonally L and turn L through a gate in the bottom corner of the second field. In August 2004 the enclosure on the L held a small herd of fallow deer. Turn L before a footbridge that leads to Old House, then cross a stile and turn R along the fence to the second gate and turn L on the house drive. Go through a gate on the L and follow the waymark posts to a stile and turn L on a path. Cross a stile and before reaching Slythehurst again turn R over a stile and

head up the RH side of a field to the B2127. 3. Bear R across the road to a fingerpost and a narrow path between gardens, then beside a fence. Turn R behind a garage block, then turn L across the drive to Sayers Croft Rural Centre. Cross a stile and go along the LH side of a recreation ground. Turn R along the bottom fence and at the next corner turn L on a path. At a 'T' junction turn R and at a road turn L uphill. The Church of St Peter and St Paul on the Mount dates from 1140 and has been nicely restored after the tower and chancel collapsed in the 1830's. The nave and south door are original. Cross the road from the church to a path beside the school. When the tarmac drive turns R you continue forward on the grass with a hedge on your R to a stile in the corner. Turn R over a second stile and on over 2 more to join a drive. At Shippen Hill turn R back to the pub.

Fallow Deer Stag

The Windmill, Ewhurst.

In August 2004, during the last minute check carried out to try to field any significant pub changes before publication, we discovered that The Windmill had been converted into a wine bar and restaurant with no real ale. There were "House Rules" taped to the doors.

Customers should recognise that the establishment was 'dedicated to fine dining'. No dogs, no wet clothing or footwear, no children unless dining, which is unlikely with no bar snacks and no main courses under £10. The dress code is smart casual, so who do you know who goes walking in a cashmere cardy and Gucci loafers? In this traditional walkers' pub nestling beneath Pitch Hill with superb views from the conservatory and terraced garden, walkers are now being actively discouraged.

The charming barmaid from Oz listened politely to my rantings, and said they might cater for walkers later by installing tables on decking in the garden, with an adjacent barbecue. Nice in winter. Perhaps they will install an outside toilet for us at the same time? Needless to say that on a bright sunny day they had no lunchtime customers. As this is such excellent walking country I decided against deleting the walk. The restaurant seems doomed to fail as "the wrong place in the wrong place" and by the time you do the walk a change for the better may have occurred. You can always do the walk from Hurtwood Control car park No. 3 (see map) and lunch at any one of the pubs featured in Walks 12, 21 or 34, all of which are only 5 minutes drive away. The latest status of The Windmill can be obtained by telephone: 01483 277566.

The Windmill is on the Shere road about 1 mile north of Ewhurst centre. Turn south off the A25 signed Shere and follow signs for Ewhurst for 4 miles. There is parking at the pub or in a Hurtwood Control car park nearby – see map.

Approx distance of walk 4¾ miles. Start at OS Map Ref : TQ 080424.

If you go down in the woods of Winterfold Forest today you will be sure of not one but two big surprises as you suddenly come upon superb views over first the S. Downs and later the N. Downs. A good all weather walk perhaps best at bluebell time or in autumn for the colours. The walk may be combined with Walk 34, the common point being the Ewhurst windmill in Section 1 and with Walk 21 at Mayorhouse Farm in Section 2.

1. Turn L out of the pub. Opposite the entrance to Hurtwood Control Car Park No. 3 turn L into a drive and through a small gate waymarked GW (Greensand Way). Go uphill and bear L round Ewhurst windmill. At a fork keep ahead on the footpath (GW). Keep ahead over 2 crossing tracks and bear half L over a road junction into Hurtwood Control Car Park No. 4. Take the path behind the notice board up Reynards Hill and at a fork go L up to a bench seat for a glorious view to the S. Downs. Bear R back to the main path following the GW. At a fork keep L on a path lined with hurts or bilberry bushes and sweet chestnuts, the first of many on this walk. Just before a road turn L on a crossing path. Reach the road again and in 50 yards turn R at a bridleway fingerpost. At a fork keep L and before a gate turn L, then fork R on a bridleway downhill.
2. Fork L to pass beside Winterfold Cottage and turn R down the drive. Cross a road and

continue on a bridleway. Just before this goes downhill cross a stile on the R to a parallel footpath with Helmet Copse to your R. Pass a gate on the L and turn L on a crossing track leading uphill to Mayorhouse Farm. Pass the first farm building on the R then turn R over a stile by a gate and through the stable yard. Pass the barn with a dovecote above and bear R at a fingerpost onto a track with fine views to the N. Downs. Pass a waymarked stile and continue to another stile in a hedge. Cross the bridleway to 2 more stiles, then cross a field to a fenced path. At Winterfold Lane turn L past the timber framed Shophouse Farm. In a few yards turn R over a stile and between fields. Cross another lane into a drive (fingerpost removed in 2004). Pass to the L of buildings and down steps into woods. Cross a footbridge and turn L on a crossing track and L again on a drive.

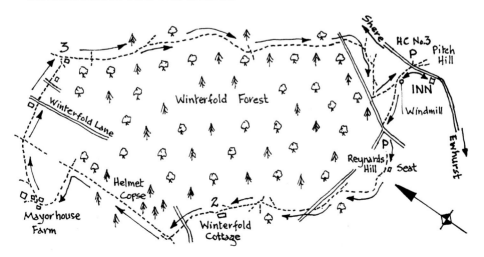

3. In 15 yards turn R round a cottage onto a waymarked bridleway that leads for over 1 mile through Winterfold Forest. At a fork keep R and eventually reach a major path junction. Maintain direction uphill on a wide track and continue when this meets a gravelled forest road, still uphill. Pass to the L of an electric gate and cross a road to a footpath that bends R. Turn R at 2 'T' junctions and at a fork go R back to the road, where turn L on the drive to Four Winds. Take the path beside the gate that you started out on and turn R at the bottom back to the pub.

Collins Farm, Walk No 14

Waterland Farm, Walks Nos 14 and 29

The Parrot Inn, Forest Green.

This attractive old inn, ideally situated opposite the village green and with extensive gardens, has been sympathetically extended to provide a restaurant, function room, games and TV areas without detracting from the character of the bar. This has comfortable banquette window seats and houses a lovely old fireplace and a grand brass and copper parrot on a swing. They are even licensed for weddings if you really fall in love with the place.

The pub is open all day from 11am, Sun 12 noon, and food is served all day from 12 noon.

The ales include their own Parrot, brewed by Hogs Back, Hogs Back TEA, London Pride and Courage Best.

The menu has baguettes, jackets and ploughman's and more imaginative offerings such as Lake Victoria perch with mango curry sauce, crab, fennel and orange salad, red onion and mixed pepper tart, vegetable balti, duck with roast parsnips, pork Stroganoff and scallops with Parmesan and pine nut tart. There is a children's menu and a play area in the garden. Dogs are welcome in the bar.

Tel: 01306 621339.

Walk No. 14

The Parrot is in the centre of Forest Green facing the extensive village green. The village is on the B2127 between Ewhurst and Ockley. It may be reached from the A25 by turning south on the B2126 at Abinger Hammer for 4 miles through Holmbury St Mary. There is ample parking at the pub.

Approx distance of walk 4½ miles. Start at OS Map Ref : TQ 124413.

A pleasant walk over farmland and through woods south of Holmbury Hill and Leith Hill with good views in places and limited hill climbing. One bridleway may be very messy in winter. The walk may be combined with Walk 29 near the start and with Walk 18 at Point 3.

1. Turn L out of the pub. Just past the village pond turn R on the drive to Pond Cottage and turn R on a grass path before the gate. After the third sleeper bridge bear L to a lane and turn L. Pass Brookfield and reach a point where the lane bends R in front of a power pole with a stile on the L. (From here to the next waymark post on the L is the start of Section 3 of Walk 29 in reverse. If you wish to combine the two, Walk 29 goes L over the stile.) Continue up the lane towards Waterland Farm and turn R onto a footpath about 15 yards before the first barn. Cross a footbridge, then a stile, and bear R to another stile. Do not cross it but continue round the fence to a stile in the field corner. Cross a footbridge and go up a lawn to a fingerpost and along a drive. Forest Hill Church can be seen on the R with Leith Hill ahead. Turn L on the road, then R into Mill Lane. At a waymarked crossing

track turn L. Cross a stile and maintain direction along the RH side of a field. At a fingerpost turn R across a field and bear L at the next fingerpost. Cross a stile by a fingerpost and bear half L to a stile and footbridge to the R of a chicken run. Continue between gardens to a road.

2. Cross to a fingerpost and stile and continue along the LH side of a field and then 80 yards along the bottom of the field to a stile. Follow the waymark along the RH side of a meadow and turn L through a gateway, following the waymark along the LH side of a field and round to a stile in the corner in holly bushes. Turn L along the fence and into woods. Bear R up to a stile and fingerpost that points you half L up a sloping field. There is no path but maintain direction over the brow of the hill and down to Upfolds Farm. Pass between the farm buildings and turn R past a small building on brick pillars.

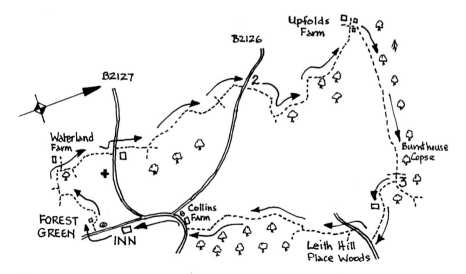

44

(The bridleway sign is on the back of the building.) Continue to a footbridge and turn R on a wide sandy track that doubles as a mud slide after heavy rain. This goes gradually uphill in woodland. At a 4 fingered post take the uphill path ahead and in 40 yards reach a fork.

3. If you go L uphill at the fork for 200 yards you will reach point 2 of Walk 18. For this walk fork R on a footpath that winds through woodland. Go down 2 flights of steps, turn R on a grass path, then L up more steps. The path skirts round a garden and emerges on a road via a kissing gate. Turn R, then at a barrier turn L into Leith Hill Place woods. In a few yards fork R

downhill. Keep ahead at a National Trust waymark. About 40 yards before the track bends L at the next National Trust waymark make your way over a ditch to the fence on the R and continue beside it. At the end of the field on the R follow the waymark into a small bluebell copse. The path bends R to a waymarked sleeper bridge into the meadow beyond. Bear half L across the meadow to a waymark post then bear R through another small copse to a stile. Turn L along the field edge to 2 stiles. Keep beside the fence on the L down the field and along the bottom to a stile leading out to a road. Turn R and bear L past Collins Farm and goose pond back to the pub.

View South from Burnthouse Copse

The Compasses, Gomshall.

Try saying 'God Encompasseth' after a pint or twelve and you will know why the name was soon corrupted to Goat and Compasses and eventually to just The Compasses. Situated beside the Tillingbourne with bridges over to the beer garden and separated from the 11th century Gomshall Mill by a pack horse bridge, this must have been an idyllic spot before it was polluted by the constant traffic on the A25.

Even so it is still a fine inn where, thanks to an old Gibbs Mew lease, the 4 real ales are changed regularly and the mass produced, taste reduced outpourings of the major breweries never get a look-in. On our visit Tom Woods' Bomber County, Exmoor Wild Cat, Shepheard Neame Spitfire and Wychwood Shires demonstrated the refinement of the landlord's taste buds.

The standard is maintained in the comprehensive menu covering sandwiches and snacks, "meals for little people", vegetarian dishes, staple main courses including home-made pies and an imaginative specials board specialising in delicious fish dishes.

The inn is open all day every day and serves food from noon to 9pm, welcomes children and dogs and has a few en-suite rooms if you cannot bear to tear yourself away.

Tel: 01483202506.

The Compasses is situated in the centre of Gomshall on the A25 just west of the railway arch. There is parking beside the pub and Gomshall station is nearby.

Approx distance of walk 4¼ miles. Start at OS Map Ref : TQ 085479.

A hilly exercise walk mainly in woodland including a mile of the N. Downs Way,with bluebells in season and much wildlife. The walk passes the Abinger Arms (Walk 1) so those with Grand Old Duke of York syndrome could march up to the top of the hill and down again twice to make a longer walk. If you have the OS map you could design your own combination of the two walks.

1. Turn L out of the pub and cross the road. Twenty yards beyond the petrol station turn R at a fingerpost on a path up Netley Down. Continue uphill through woods with gardens over to the R at first. At a fork follow the waymark to the R and at a 'T' junction turn R. Pass a barrier and at the next 'T' junction turn L on a bridleway uphill. At a fork go R and a wide track comes in from the R before you reach the waymarked N Downs Way crossing track.

2. Turn R along the ND Way for 1 mile through scatterings of bluebells. Pass a Little Kingswood notice board on the R. At a waymarked fork the ND Way goes R but you keep ahead. Go over a wide crossing track and ignore a L turn. Pass 2 metal gates and in 100 yards turn R on a bridleway signed with a red waymark uphill through massed bluebells. At a 'T' junction turn R and soon cross the ND Way. A brief detour

onto Blatchford Down to the R here affords fine views. This point is common to Walk 1.

3. Continue downhill on this path ignoring L and R turns. The path flattens between fields that are often full of pheasants and then crosses the railway line. Pass Hackhurst Farm on the L and keep ahead on the surfaced Hackhurst Lane to reach the A25 beside the Abinger Arms at Abinger Hammer. Cross the road carefully, turn R along the A25 and opposite the Grade 1 listed Hunters' Moon Farm turn L at a fingerpost onto a bridleway. Cross a bridge over the R Tillingbourne and with a gate ahead take the bridle path next to it. Bear R past houses and at a 'T' junction turn R on a track. Ignore a bridle path on the L past Twiga Lodge and re cross the river. Back at the A25 turn L under a railway arch and continue past Gomshall Mill, now incorporated into a restaurant and back to the pub.

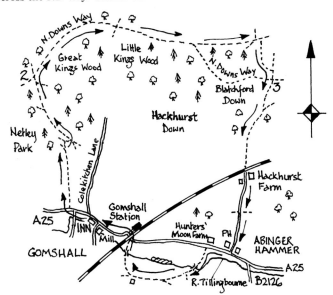

The Royal Oak, Great Bookham.

The Royal Oak is a small friendly 2 bar local. The building dates from the 16th century and records show that in 1628 they paid a rent of one red rose and a quart of lampreys (eels) to the Manor of Eastwick. To be used in a witch's spell no doubt. Evidence of age is to be seen in the old beams and inglenook fireplace. Ginger, who dresses in combat gear and collects weapons and frequents the public bar, says this is the best pub in Bookham and he had plenty to say about the others.

The ales are Abbot, Adnams, Tetleys and Bass and there is a choice of 8 wines by the glass.

The menu is comprehensive and very reasonably priced. Snacks such as baguettes, jackets, goujons, tachos and ploughman's are available and main courses include steak and chicken 'combos', scampi, curry, chicken parmegnane, penne pasta, lasagne, fajitas, fish and chips and gammon steak. Outside there are 2 tables by the front entrance and 6 in the small rear garden. Children and dogs under control are welcome.

The pub is open all day Mon-Sat from 11am-11pm and Sun 12-10.30pm. Food is served 12-3pm, Sundays 2-6pm.

Tel: 01372 452533.

Great Bookham is on the A246 west of Leatherhead. The Royal Oak is in the High Street, a turning off the A246. There is a small car park at the pub or nearby – see map.

Approx distance of walk 5 miles. Start at OS Map Ref : TQ 135545.

The walk may be combined with Walk 9 and with Walk 38 as all three pass through Point 2. Part of Section 1 and Goldstone Farm can be very muddy after rain and boots are strongly recommended. A gently undulating walk on farmland and through woods around the National Trust's Polesden Lacey. It would be a shame not to visit when you are passing the door. Tel 01372 455031.

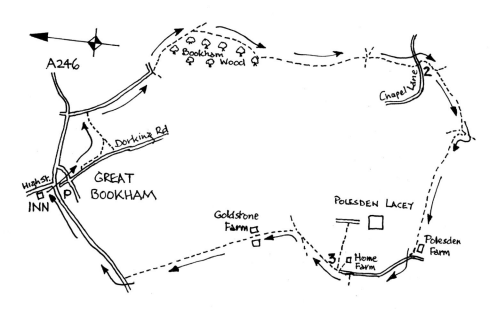

1. Turn R out of the pub and cross the A246 at the traffic lights. Turn R for a few yards then L to a road. At crossroads go ahead into Dorking Rd. Keep to the LH side and then beside the hedge in Chrystie Recreation Ground. At the second field go diagonally L then R past tennis courts and turn L on a path to reach a 'T' junction, where turn R on a residential road. This is Downs View Rd. Where it bends L cross to a bridleway. Go over one crossing path, then another past a seat and a fine view to the L. Bookham Wood, full of bluebells in season is to your R. Ignore a R turn and at a fork go R still beside the wood. In the field corner go forward under power lines and bear L into woods, then beside a fence. There is a view to the R briefly of Ranmore Common with the spire of Ranmore Church on the horizon. Continue downhill over a way-marked crossing path. Ignore a LH fork and grass paths to the L and R and cross a field via 2 gates.

2. Cross Chapel Lane to the bridleway opposite. This is Point 2 on both Walk 9 and Walk 38. At a fork by a barn go R through a gate and up a long field to another gate. Turn L and in 40 yards turn R through a gate and bear R to a fingerpost, where turn L signed Polesden Valley Walk. Follow NT waymarks through fields and a bluebell wood, past a small pond and then Polesden Farm. At a 'T' junction above the farm turn L then R to a lane uphill. Follow the lane round to the R and under a thatched bridge. There are soon fine views ahead. Just past the entrance to Home Farm House, if you want to visit Polesden Lacey turn R through

Walk No. 16

a gate and across a field to the main drive. Otherwise go ahead on a stony track. A public byway comes in from the L and in 10 yards turn L on a road that leads through Goldstone Farm. We were fortunate to see a redstart in the farmyard. Maintain direction between 2 fields. It was here that the Harry Potter of the family decided to have an experiment. He got his brothers and sister and grandparents all unsuspecting to hold hands. Then he touched the electric fence. This was fun for all except for Granny who acted as the earth! The merri-

ment was swiftly curtailed when a wretch secreted in a hide on the L shot a passing collared dove out of the air above us. Why is there never a hand grenade to be found when you need one? It beggars belief but the Countryside Alliance organises dove shooting holidays in Argentina. Spreading the gospel of wild life butchery worldwide. Get down from soap box and at the A246 cross over and turn R along the pavement for half a mile, then turn L up High Street back to the pub.

Highland Cattle, Headley Heath, Walk No 17

The Cock Horse, Headley.

Due to its proximity to Box Hill, Nower Wood and the heather clad expanses of Headley Heath, the spacious Cock Inn had long been a favourite hostelry with walkers and cyclists. Then, during the nineteen nineties, an owner suffering from over developed sensibilities and general confusion changed the name to The Cock Horse. It is a long way from Banbury Cross and the illustration on the inn sign is of plough horses.

When Six Continents took charge they closed the public bar, originally a bakehouse and dating from the 16th century. They also introduced fast food style illustrated plastic menus and for a time in early 2004 this was a pub with no draught ale. On our latest visit just prior to publication in May 2004 there had just been another change of ownership and the pub was on offer as a franchise. In the circumstances a review cannot be offered. There are no other pubs near enough to re route the walk unless as a longer ramble combined with Walk 25. This walk is too good to miss but it would be sensible to telephone for up to date details of opening times and refreshment offerings before setting out.

Tel: 01372 377258.

If all else fails the pubs featured in Walks 9, 10, 24 and 25 are all within 10 minutes drive of the Cock Horse.

Walk No. 17

Headley is on the B2033 and is reached by turning E off the A24 onto Reigate Rd at Leatherhead or N from the A25 onto the B2032 at Betchworth. The pub is in the centre of the village next to the church and has a large car park.

Approx distance of Walk 4 miles. Start at OS Map Ref : TQ 205548.

Commencing through farmland this hilly walk visits nature reserves and a bluebell wood and gives fine views over the downs before returning across Headley Heath where stonechats chat and Highland cattle graze. Not recommended after rain due to one steep decline on chalk. The walk may be combined with Walk 25 at Section 2.

1. From the pub patio cross the road to the bus stop and take the footpath between fields. At a road turn R into a side road and, opposite the first house, turn L on a grass path. Fork R and at a road, Tumber St., turn R passing the 16th century Slough Farm on the L. At a junction turn L on Langley Lane. A gate on the R leads to the Nower Wood Nature Reserve. It belongs to the Surrey Wildlife Trust. Tel : 01372 379509 for details of access arrangements. You can see the bluebells from the gate and this lovely wood extends over many acres and ponds, one with a bird hide. At the end of the lane cross a road to a fingerpost and turn R on a track to a car park.

2. This is point 3 of Walk 25. Take the LH bridleway. There are bluebells to the R and you continue past a signed bridleway to emerge at the end of Mickleham Down. The spire of Ranmore Church is visible directly ahead. Having enjoyed the view, the wildflowers and the butterflies, just beyond the Mickleham Down sign step over the wire fence on the L and take the unsigned grass path on the L going downhill steeply through Cockshot Wood, a nature reserve. At a 'T' junction overlooking a field turn L. Go through a car park and cross the road past Cockshot Cottage to a signed bridleway uphill. Pass some old ramparts and at a waymark post turn sharp L downhill. The last section of this steep path is on exposed chalk and lethal when wet. At the bottom turn L on a wide track that sweeps round to the R and uphill across Headley Heath.

3. At a junction of 6 paths take the blue arrowed bridleway directly ahead to the L of

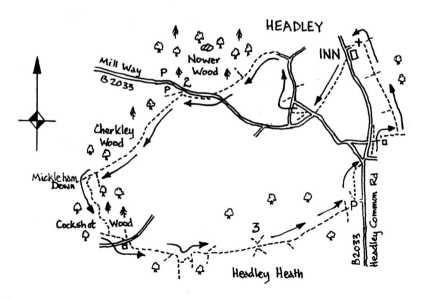

2 seats. In 30 yards at a fork go L through a gate. Follow this path past a lone silver birch. Woodlarks nest on the ground here so dogs should be kept on leads during the nesting season. At other times highland cattle graze in this enclosure. Exit through another gate and on to a car park. Turn L through the car park to a path between grass mounds. Bear L, then R through gorse ignoring 2 minor side paths. At a fork before a large gorse bush go R and R again at the next 2 forks to reach Headley Common Rd. Cross over and turn R down a private road to a waymark post and turn L on the bridleway running parallel to the road. At a fork by a fingerpost turn R on a drive to a house, then turn L over a stile before the gate. Keep to the RH side of a field, then turn L before a stile, now facing Headley Church. Maintain direction towards it over several meadows and stiles, then turn L through the churchyard and back to the pub.

Leith Hill Tower, Walk No 18

The King's Head, Holmbury St Mary.

The King's Head is a free house and has been a pub since 1835 when the ale was brewed on the premises. The ales are still a strong feature with the excellent Ringwood and Horsham Best bitters augmented by Old Speckled Hen, Greene King IPA and guests, e.g. Kings Red River and Old and Greene King Mild.

A change of ownership in 2003 brought some innovations in the menu with platters 'for two to share' featuring nachos, whitebait, enchiladas, scampi and chicken goujons, etc. Traditional fare such as beef and ale pie, cod and chips, sirloin and rib eye steaks, ham egg and chips and liver and bacon is available and there is a good selection of baguettes and tortilla wraps. This can all be consumed at tables in the bar or in the rear restaurant or the attractive garden with a fine view to Pasture Wood. In 2004 the barman had a penchant for loud music. As a consequence customers had to raise their voices to hold a conversation. On our visit a large party of walkers had been driven out by the noise level and the flashing lights of a games machine and were heading for the Royal Oak as we arrived. Personally I think it should be compulsory for all pubs who find it necessary to play music at lunchtimes to be issued with compilation tapes of Frank Sinatra, Ella Fitzgerald, Nat King Cole and Billie Holiday to be played at a controlled volume! Failing that a polite request to turn it down usually meets with the desired response and proved to be the case here.

The pub is open all day every day from noon and lunchtime food is served to 2.30pm. Dogs and well behaved children are welcome.

Tel: 01306 730282.

To reach Holmbury St Mary from the A25, take the B2126 south from Abinger Hammer and follow signs for just over 2 miles. Pass the church on the R and take the next turning on the R. The Kings Head is on your L. There is limited parking in front of the pub or in the street.

Approx distance of walk 4½ miles. Start at OS Map Ref : TQ 112442.

A lovely woodland walk following the Greensand Way to the top of Leith Hill with minimal effort and returning over Wotton Common. Nice views all round from the top. A good one for autumn for the colours in the beech woods. Muddy in places in winter. The walk may be combined with Walk 14 at Point 2.

1. Turn L out of the pub, then L at a 'T' junction and R on the B2126. Take the first L, Pasturewood Rd, and in 200 yards as it bends L turn R on the signed Greensand Way (GW). At a fork keep L on the undulating higher path and ignore all side paths. Maintain direction past High Ashes Farm and turn R at a 'T' junction. In 50 yards at a fork go L (GW) and at the next fork keep ahead R (GW) to reach a 'T' junction.

2. If you want to combine the two walks go R here for 200 yards to Point 3 of Walk 14. To continue this walk turn L to reach Leith Hill Rd. Cross over and follow the fingerpost signed 'The Tower'. Stay on this wide path to reach the summit of Leith Hill and the Tower. For opening times telephone the National Trust warden on 01306 711774. Continue past the tower for 30 yards to the National Trust sign, where turn L with a barrier to your L. At a crossing path turn L and at the next crossing path turn R downhill. At a fork go R and ignore minor side turnings. You may have to negotiate

a small pond in the path, then at a fork go L. At a 'T' junction turn R on a more substantial track. Where the track splits into three, take the LH path up to a road.

3. Bear half L to a fingerpost, through woods and across a field to a kissing gate. Continue on a fenced path past gardens on the L, cross over a wide waymarked crossing path and take the LH of 2 paths up to Leith Hill Rd. Cross to a fingerpost and maintain direction past a 4 fingered post, now with a field on your L. Cross a stile and continue down the LH side of a field to a gate. In 15 yards cross a stile on the R, bear L for 20 yards to a grass track, then turn R on a waymarked footpath that winds through woods. At a waymark post bear L and at the next waymark fork R, soon through rhododendron bushes. Go over a waymarked crossing path and at the next waymark turn R, then fork L to Pasturewood Rd. Turn L and retrace your outward steps back to the pub.

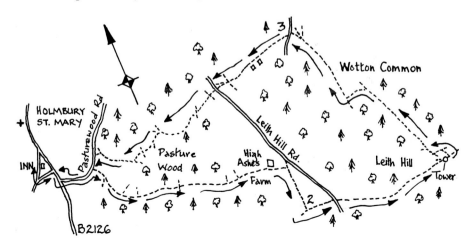

The Jolly Farmer, Horne.

The Jolly Farmer started life in the 15th century as 2 cottages and a cowshed before being converted into a pub in 1788. On our first visit it was awaiting a new pub sign so we had to return for the photograph. It turned out to be a ruddy faced farmer on a tractor replacing the old Breueghel style drunken farmer and peasant wench. In my experience changes for the better in inn signage are as rare as hens' teeth and this is no exception. A review of the pub in 1976 was also critical of the then sign as follows: "the farmer on this inn-sign appears to be more demented than jolly and there is some controversy about what he is going to do with that cow!" So we know why that one was changed.

This is a friendly comfortable local with exposed beams, an open fire in the public bar and a log burning stove in the rustic yet pink painted "Parlour and Private Bar". On our last visit in April 2004 the landlord had expunged the pink paint but was busy covering other walls with lavender. He has a photograph taken with Jack Charlton on the wall, not a man who frequently drinks in lavender painted pubs I would have thought. Maybe the colour was selected by Joanna Lumley whose photograph is also on the wall?

The menu is limited but excellent value, e.g. succulent beef stir fry and a generous prawn salad. In 2004 Thai dishes were introduced with a choice of 5 daily lunchtime specials. Snacks include sandwiches, home-made soup, breaded crab claws and burgers. The ales are Sussex, with a choice of the brews from Harveys or Hall and Woodhouse made to the Old King and Barnes recipe, or Courage Best. Children and dogs are welcome and there is a small garden at the rear.

Hours are Mon-Fri 12-3pm and 5.30-11pm; weekends open all day from noon. No food on Tuesday evenings.

Tel: 01342 842867.

The Jolly Farmer can be reached from Blindley Heath by turning west off the A22 on Byers Lane for 1 mile then turn R on Whitewood Lane. From the A25 turn south in Bletchingly on Outwood Lane and in Outwood turn L on Gayhouse Lane, then L on Whitewood Lane. There is ample parking at the pub.

Approx distance of walk 4 miles. Start at OS Map Ref : TQ 348451.

A walk on rolling farmland with fine views., mostly on bridleways with easy route finding. Skylarks sing overhead and there are attractive properties to admire. The walk may be combined with Walk 32 at Point 3.

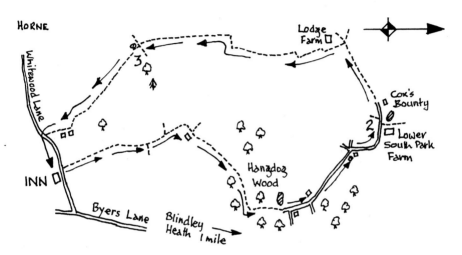

1. Cross the road from the pub to a wide bridleway. Stay on this for ½ mile ignoring a stile on the R. At a fork go R through a gate. Pass a house on the R ignoring the stile to your L. Continue between fields and through a gate into Hangdog Wood. Keep on this track eventually passing a pond in a garden on the L. At a junction keep L ahead past Paddock Wood and at the next fork go L past Whitewalls. The lane bends R, then L to the lovely Lower South Park Farm.

2. A footpath goes through here and it is worth walking in as far as the pond if only to reinforce your resolve to buy a lottery ticket each week. While gawping here we were further excited when a female ring ouzel alighted on the fence in front of us. I had never seen one in Surrey before. Back on the track the neighbouring Cox's Bounty may pose a question for local historians. Was Mr Cox a sea captain who captured a foreign treasure ship and did his share of the resultant bounty finance the building of this sturdy cottage? Continue to a waymarked junction by the gate to Lodge Farm and turn L through a gate onto a path between fences. This joins a farm track, where turn L for ¾ mile along the RH edge of large fields. Remember to look back for good views and listen out for skylarks.

3. Go through a waymarked gate and over a crossing track to a stile by a small pond. This section is common to Walk 32. Bear half L across a meadow to a footbridge and maintain direction over another meadow with fine views ahead. Follow the waymark across the next field, cross a footbridge and follow a fenced path. Turn R on a drive and at Whitewood Lane turn L away from Walk 32 and back to the pub.

The Running Horse, Leatherhead.

The Running Horse has been an inn since 1520 and has interesting architectural features and memorabilia on the walls. Queen Elizabeth I is reputed to have stayed here when the River Mole was in flood and her coach was unable to cross. Henry VIII's poet laureate John Skelton, wrote a poem about the pub and a lady called Elynore Rummynge. The pub was named Rummings House after this inspirational landlady until the present name was adopted. Among her many attributes "she breweth moppy ale" and sold it "to travellers to tynkers, to sweters, to swynkers and all good drinkers." Good girl! And Skelton was obviously a poet after, or rather before, Betjeman's own heart.

Moppy ale, or perhaps hoppy ale, it was then; now there is a choice of 6 including, on our visit, Timothy Taylor's, The Landlord. I confess I paid little attention to the other 5 but I think they included London Pride and Youngs bitter.

This is a busy town pub, deservedly popular with office workers who spill into the compact suntrap garden in summer. The menu is comprehensive and reasonably priced. There is a good choice of sandwiches, jackets, 'toasted melts', burgers, omelettes, nachos, popular main courses and a daily specials board, The service is friendly and efficient and the quality of the food and the cooking is a match for other nearby pubs that charge more for the same meal. Best of all they serve until 3pm and you can pre-order. Children are welcome except in the public bar. Dogs are welcome to come and meet the 2 residents.

Opening hours are : Mon-Sat 11am-11pm, Sun 12-10.30pm. Sunday lunch is served from 12-6pm.

Tel: 01372 372081.

The Running Horse is in Bridge Street, Leatherhead, close to the eastern end of the bridge and about ¼ mile south of the railway station. There is limited parking at the pub and the alternative we used was the public car park at Bocketts Farm, signed from the roundabout on the A246 – see Map. You can start the walk from there.

Approx distance of walk 5¼ miles. Start at OS Map Ref : TQ 164564 (the pub) or TQ 156550(the farm).

A nice all weather stroll on dry paths over Fetcham Downs and Norbury Park with fine views and beside the R Mole. It can be combined with Walk 24 from Point 3 – see text.

1. Turn R out of the pub over the bridge and turn L before the railway arch. Pass the Leisure Centre Car Park and just before the Leisure Centre fork L on a footpath, now with a sports field to your L. At a crossing track turn R signed Hawks Hill. Cross the railway bridge and bear L on the track. At a fork go R on the narrower path, soon uphill. Turn L at a fingerpost signed Young St. There are nice views to the L and skylarks sing over the fields as you drop down to cross the A246 to a bridleway.

2. Go ahead to pass between Bocketts Farm and the car park. The farm has many interesting breeds of animals, a playbarn and tea rooms and is a very popular family day out, Tel : 01372 363764. Your path ahead is signed Woodland Trail. Ignore 3 fingerposts pointing L, skirt round a barn and turn L on a wide crossing bridleway. Pass a fingerpost on the L and at the next crossing path turn L uphill on a signed bridleway into woods, soon with Norbury Park to the R. Maintain direction past side turnings and turn L at a 'T' junction. Go through a gate and fork L to pass an information board and seats. You are now on a tarmac drive and pass Norbury Park House on the R. The drive bends R and

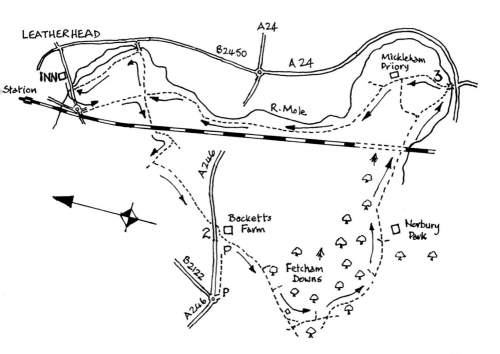

59

there are fine views across the Mole valley to Mickleham, Cherkley Court and Leatherhead. Where the drive bends sharp L go straight ahead on a signed bridleway to reach a lane.

3. To combine with Walk 24, turn R over the R Mole, cross the A24 and take the Old London Rd. The Running Horses is 200 yards on the R.

To continue this walk turn L on the lane and pass Mickleham Priory and Norbury Park Farm. Goldfinches and linnets were taking thistle seeds inches from the head of a large bull with a muddy face as we passed. The only cheese made in Surrey, called Norbury Blue, is made here in the farm dairy. It is on sale in Mickleham village. Fork L out of the farmyard through a way-marked gate. Turn R at a finger post by Lilac Cottage, signed to Leatherhead. Keep on this path across fields beside the R Mole. Go under a bridge, through a gate, then the path bears L away from the river. At a crossing track turn R signed Gimcrack Hill and rejoin the river. Turn L on a footpath before the bridge. This is the nicest section of river bank with an attractive old bridge and many water birds including herons and wagtails by the weir. Turn R over the road bridge back to the pub.

Norbury Park House

River Mole

William IV, Little London.

The pub has its origins in the 14th century and for a while was named after Garibaldi. The simple bar with ancient inglenook fireplace in operation is a welcoming place after a winter walk.

Being a free house, there are 5 ales to choose from – Hogs Back TEA and Hop Garden Gold, Abbot, Flowers IPA and Bass.

Deservedly featured in the Good Pub and Good Beer Guides, the pub and garden are frequently overflowing in summer. The menu offers a good selection of sandwiches, including steak and hot salt beef and economy snacks like a bowl of cheesy chips. Main courses include gammon steak, broccoli, leek and stilton crumble, vegetarian quiche and daily specials such as succulent pork chops and rib eye steaks. You can have your cod and chips to eat in or take away. Dogs are welcome in the bar and children in the dining area but not vice versa. There is a small restaurant upstairs.

Opening hours are Mon-Sat 11am-3pm and 5.30-11pm; Sun 12-3pm and 7-10.30pm. The kitchen is closed Sunday and Monday evenings.

Tel: 01483 202685.

Walk No. 21

The William IV is in Little London, the eastern boundary of Albury Heath, 1 mile S.W of Shere. From the A25 turn south on the A248, Albury Street, take the first left, New Rd, first left again, Park Rd, and first right, Little London. There is parking behind the pub and on Albury Heath – see map.

Approx distance of walk 5¾ miles. Start at OS Map Ref : TQ 066467.

A walk commencing on farmland with views to the N Downs and continuing in woodland over Farley Heath, Blackheath and Albury Heath. The route is mostly on bridleways, where there are likely to be muddy sections in winter. The walk may be combined with Walk 13, the common point being in Section 2 between Shophouse Farm and Mayorhouse Farm.

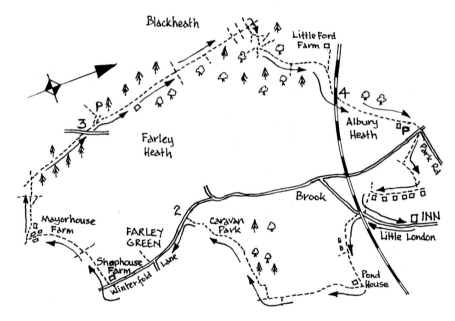

1. Turn R out of the pub, pass under a railway arch and turn L into a lane, the drive to Pond Farm. At the end enter the drive to Pond House and cross a stile on the L. Exit over another stile and turn R on a track. After ½ mile turn R over a stile beside a gate. The path bends L, then R and goes uphill to a stile into a caravan park. In 50 yards at a fingerpost turn L up steps and follow a succession of fingerposts and waymarks through the site and out over a stile onto a fenced path. Go through a kissing gate into a field and bear half L to another kissing gate in the middle of the bottom fence.

2. Turn L on a road and at a fork keep R signed to Winterfold. The footpath on the R here was guarded by a bull of Papal propor-

tions, so continue down the road as far as the timber framed Shophouse Farm on the R. Past the gate turn R over a stile onto a fenced path. Continue over a field and 2 stiles, then across a sunken bridleway and up steps to another stile. Go ahead on a track that bears left through the barns and stables of Mayorhouse Farm. Turn R out of the gate and pass the farmhouse on the R. Ignore a waymarked path on the R and a minor crossing path, then at the next wide crossing path turn R. At a fork keep ahead L to reach a road.

3. Cross over past a fingerpost and maintain direction, passing a Hurtwood Control notice on your L, then immediately fork R. Stay on this sandy bridleway ignoring side paths through chestnut trees and past a

house on the R. The path widens and you go over a wide crossing path. Pass a field on the R, and at a waymarked crossing path keep ahead. At a fork with a gate to your L keep L ahead. Continue over a waymarked crossing path, then another (post 230/232), and at the third waymark turn R. At a waymarked fork go L and at the next fork go R to reach a clearing where 6 paths meet. Bear half R to post no. 235. Do not take the path adjacent to the post, take the one on the immediate L that soon becomes sunken. It may be muddy but you should be able to find an alternative parallel route above. At post 237

keep ahead L to pass Little Ford Farm over to the L. Your path joins the drive from the farm and becomes a track.

4. Go under a railway arch and continue uphill to reach a sports field. Pass the changing rooms and a car park and at a fork go R to a road junction. Cross over and take the footpath to the R of the Park Road sign. At a 'T' junction turn L on a track and at the next junction turn R passing houses on your L. After the last house turn L on a crossing track, then fork L at a waymark onto a narrow footpath downhill and turn L on the road back to the pub.

Shophouse Farm

The Mint Arms, Lower Kingswood.

The first thing that strikes you about The Mint Arms freehouse is the amazing collection of all things copper and brass that hangs from the ceiling. The comfortable central bar has a games area with pool table, darts and TV on one side and a recently refurbished restaurant on the other. Outside is a nice garden and an exceptionally well equipped play area for children.

The ales are Hogs Back TEA, Flowers IPA, London Pride and Bass.

The snack menu is outstanding with a choice of 11 fillings for baguettes and sandwiches, plain and toasted, 8 omelettes, 5 salads and "wood fired" pizzas to eat in or take a way. You can also order a "mixed combo" of starters. Main courses include "surf and turf", mixed grill, poached salmon, steak and kidney pudding, breaded plaice, various steaks and Jamaican jerk-chicken breast in Caribbean spices. Children and dogs on leads are welcome but no dogs in the garden.

The pub is open all day from 11am-11pm, Sun 12-10.30pm. Food is served to 2.30pm and all day Sunday but not on Monday evenings. Large groups are invited to telephone orders in advance when tables will be reserved.

Tel: 01737 242957.

The Mint Arms at Lower Kingswood is reached by turning west off the A217 into Stubbs Lane just over ½ mile north of M25 junction 8, then turn L at the cross-roads into Buckland Rd. There is parking at the pub.

Approx distance of walk 5½ miles. Start at OS Map Ref : TQ 248532.

This is a lovely walk mostly on National Trust land on the N Downs Way and Pilgrims' Way with stunning views in places, particularly from Colley Hill, where Shetland cattle graze and ending through the pretty Margery bluebell wood. Chalk paths may be slippery after rain and there is one fairly stiff climb up Colley Hill. The walk may be combined with Walk 26 at Point 2.

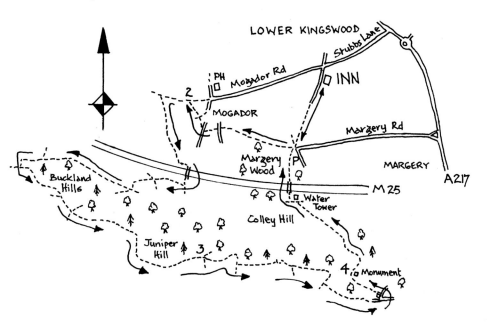

1. Turn L out of the pub and maintain direction when the tarmac ends. Just before Margery Wood car park turn R at a finger-post on a bridleway beside the bluebell wood. Pass under the boughs of larch trees, beautiful in spring and there are more blue-bells before you cross a road. At a fork keep L and at the next road turn R, signed Banstead Heath. Just past a waymark post fork L off the road onto a bridleway, cross another unmade road and continue on a signed bridleway. At a 'T' junction turn L, signed Chequers Lane.

2. The next section to the notice board is common to Walk 26. At a 4 fingered post just past a notice board turn L, signed M25 crossing ¼ mile. Follow the path and cross the motorway and at a fingerpost turn R on

a road. Continue past another fingerpost and across a bridleway, then turn L before Mulberry Cottage onto a fenced bridleway. At a 4 fingered post in front of Coneybury Heights turn R on a bridleway. There is a fine show of wood anemones here in April and later bluebells when the fenced path enters woodland. Emerge from the woods to a glorious view to Box Hill. Ignore a path on the R and at a gate turn L down steps. At the bottom turn L, soon downhill. At a way-marked fork go L joining the N Downs Way. Go over a waymarked crossing path and along the side of the hill. The path bends R past a NT sign for Juniper Hill.

3. At a 4 fingered post go over a crossing track and continue past a barrier on a foot-path, now the Pilgrims' Way. Ignore side

65

View to Box Hill

turnings and go down steps to skirt the rim of a pit. Go uphill and maintain direction at an unsigned path junction just past a vertical railway sleeper. Pass a field and gate on the L and at a 'T' junction turn R. In 50 yards fork L then L again on a wider track with houses over to the R. Go past a barrier and a NT notice and maintain direction on the road. Fork L past Hanger House, then turn L on a signed bridleway between a beech hedge and a high brick wall. Keep following this chalk path uphill past the memorial to Captain George Simpson, where there is a seat from which to enjoy the view.

4. Continue up and through a gate onto the grassy expanse of Colley Hill. Bear L with the terrace path, pass a seat on the L and fork L to another seat. In 30 yards fork R to a gap at a fence corner then bear R past a seat towards an old water tower. Black and white Shetland cattle are usually to be found grazing in this area. Turn L on a track in front of the water tower and in 25 yards turn R through a gate into Margery Wood, half of which was lost to the M25. Go over the motorway bridge and on to the car park. Go through the far gate and turn L through the 4 white posts onto the track you started out on and back to the pub.

The Feathers, Merstham.

The Feathers was a coaching inn on the London to Brighton road and still carries the original signage proclaiming it is a hotel but this free house no longer has any letting rooms. It does have comfortable seating areas all around the bar.

An imaginative menu lists sandwiches whose fillings include crayfish with lime mayo and pork and leek sausage and there is a choice of breads. Main courses include fish in Hoegaarden batter (Makes the batter orange. English real ale is better for batter!), rib eye steak, Thai noodles with tempura vegetables, char grilled tuna with lemon and lime dressing, crayfish linguini, char grilled chicken and parmesan salad and Mediterranean tomato and spinach risotto.

On our visit the ales were Bombardier, Old Speckled Hen, Green King IPA, Adnams Bitter and Bass but there are frequent changes. Well behaved children are welcome if seated. Dogs are not allowed inside. There is no garden but there are tables outside on a patio and gravel area before the large car park.

The pub is open all day every day from 12 noon with food served to 2.30pm Mon-Sat and all day Sunday.

Tel: 01737 645643.

Walk No. 23

The Feathers is in the centre of Merstham on the A23, just south of the bridge over the M25 and close to the railway station, which is passed on the walk. There is a large car park at the pub.

Approx distance of walk 4 miles. Start at OS Map Ref : TQ 290534.

Merstham has been blighted by motorways but the best bits have been preserved, albeit linked by a footbridge over the M25. This walk gets you away from the roaring traffic via the N Downs Way to fields and bluebell woods returning past the lovely church and along the pretty Quality Street. The walk may be combined with Walk 31 by a ½ mile detour from Rook Lane – see Maps.

1. Turn R out of the pub and R into Station Rd North. Cross the railway by the footbridge and turn L between fences. Just past the railway arch turn L through a gap in the fence over a track and through a kissing gate. Go up the grass bank ahead and bear R round an enclosure to cross a footbridge over the M25. Turn R over a stile and follow the path. At a fork keep L beside the fence and on uphill to a kissing gate. Turn R on the pavement and, just before Sarum on the L, turn L at a fingerpost onto the N Downs Way. Go through a tunnel under the M23. Bear R on a track uphill following waymarks through bushes and out into a field, then follow the chalk path across and up the field. Remember to look back as the views unfold.

2. At a fork near the top go L to a fingerpost, signed Tollsworth Manor ¼ mile. In front of a house turn L, then R on the drive past the lovely manor house. Keep on the drive to reach Rook Lane, where cross to a kissing gate and fingerpost. To combine with Walk 31 follow the path signed to Chaldon Church, ½ mile. For this walk turn L along the field edge beside the hedge. Cross a stile into woods and at a waymark post fork L, then at a fingerpost turn L, signed Alderstead Heath. Reach a concrete section and turn R on the grass parallel to

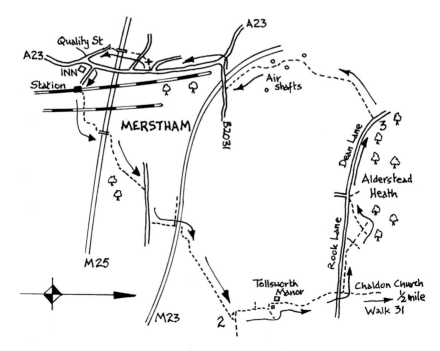

the road. At a concrete crossing track turn L, then R on Dean Lane. Pass the entrance to a Caravan Club site. The woods on the R are full of bluebells and wood anemones in April. There is no path through there so you must stay on the road for ¼ mile.

3. Opposite a fingerpost on the R turn L on a path up a field. Go through a gap and keep beside the hedge on the L. We saw a muntjac deer here. Stay with the hedge as it bends R, then L past a tall brick air shaft venting a railway tunnel below. Cross a stile passing another shaft and on downhill in woods to a stile. Cross a field to another stile by a gate and on to a road, where turn R over the M23. At a 'T' junction cross the A23 and turn L on the pavement for ¼ mile to reach St Katherine's Church. Go through the lych gate, made with timber from an old windmill and up to the church wonderfully sited on a mound in a graveyard covered in primroses in April. The church built from locally quarried stone is famous for curiosities particularly on the monuments made from odd materials and sited in unusual places. The Elinbrygge family has monuments with 16 different spellings of the surname. Sadly on our visit it was locked. Leave the churchyard via the kissing gate and on down the path to a road. Cross to a fingerpost and follow the N Downs Way over the M25 and into Quality Street. Once the Croydon road, this was renamed in the 1920s, supposedly because the actors Sir Seymour Hicks and Ellaline Terriss, who lived at The Old Forge, were appearing in the play by J.M. Barrie called Quality Street. Italian tourists were in front of The Old Forge with their cameras as we passed. A superb wisteria on the front of The Gables was the high spot of this 'chocolate box' reminder of old Merstham and The Feathers awaits on the other side of the A23.

Wood Anemones near Colley Hill, Walk 22

The Running Horses, Mickleham.

The Running Horses was a coaching inn on the old London Road from the 15th century and the main bar features a highwayman's hiding place as well as a fine inglenook fireplace. The pub name relates to the Derby of 1828 when the locals had an interest in one of the horses in a dead heat finish. Today the pub is nicely up market with a separate restaurant and bar staff in bow ties but the fundamentals of a good pub remain.

There are 4 ales, Abbot, London Pride and Adnams and Young's bitters.

Snacks include the very popular 'chunky' sandwiches, ciabatta toasties and ploughman's platters. Main courses feature various steaks, sautéed sea bass, calves livers and bacon, millefeuille of roast peppers, ricotta and pine kernels and penne pasta with chicken, spinach and pine kernels. Children under 14 are not allowed in the bar areas but there is a small patio garden at the front. Dogs are welcome and water bowls are provided.

Opening hours are Mon-Fri 11.30am-3pm and 5-11pm; weekends open all day with lunch served to 2.30pm. The pub has 5 letting rooms, one with a 4 poster. Tel: 01372 372279.

Mickleham is reached by turning east off the A24 onto the B2209 about 1½ miles south of Leatherhead. The pub is about 300 yards on the RH side opposite the church. Parking is in the streets. Box Hill station is on the route and the walk may be started from there.

Approx distance of walk 4¾ miles. Start at OS Map Ref : TQ 171534.
The walk may be combined with Walk 38 at Point 2 and Walk 25 at Point 4. Also to combine with Walk 20 see start of para 3 of Walk 20.

A strenuous walk with a bit of everything: riverside meadows, steep climbs, grassland aglow with wildflowers and butterflies in summer, cool woodland, and some very fine views. Not recommended after rain when steep slopes will be slippery.

1. Turn R out of the pub past the Church of St Michael. This is well worth a visit with a fine carved pulpit, rare Flemish stained glass and a relief of the Last Supper behind the altar. At the end of a long wall on the R turn R on a footpath, then down steps and through a kissing gate. Keep to the LH side of 2 fields to a stile and cross a lane to a narrow path that takes you down to the A24. Cross the dual carriageway through a gap in the hedge to a track. Go under the railway arch and turn L on a path. Cross a footbridge over the R Mole and continue beside the railway fence, then turn L on the road bridge past Box Hill station.
2. At the Stepping Stones pub you can combine with Walk 38, if you wish. Back at the A24 turn L and cross the road via the subway. Turn L at the other side as far as the subway sign, where turn R on a path beside the river. Keep close to the water's edge, cross a footbridge and take the path ahead signed N Downs Way. At a 'T' junction turn L and soon bear R up steps with the river below. At a fork go L, signed ND Way and

there are more steps to the R. At a 'T' junction turn R to pass the trig point and view point on the L. Just after the path enters woodland turn L on a crossing path steeply uphill, then turn R on the wider path above. At a 'T' junction turn L and through the car park opposite the entrance to Upper Farm.
3. Turn L on the road and in a few yards fork R onto a bridleway. Go over a crossing track and in a few yards at another junction take the central bridleway downhill. Stay on this path ignoring side turnings for almost 1 mile through Juniper Bottom. Cross Headley Road and take a deep breath before tackling some serious steps. At the top continue past a NT Long Walk marker post and at the next NTLW post turn L. Fork L at NTLW post no.6.
4. The next crossing path you reach is the Downs Road. If you turn R here for 350 yards you will reach Point 2 of Walk 25 should you wish to combine the walks. Otherwise cross over Downs Road and continue steeply down hill. Cross a stile and go on past the church back to the pub.

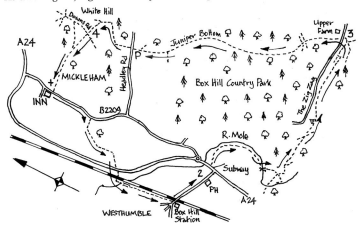

The King William IV, Mickleham.

We found the excellent King William IV free house, in the Good Pub Guide as winners of the 'Surrey Dining Pub of the Year'. Hidden away as it is I cannot imagine anybody finding it any other way, except by recommendation.

Built into a hillside with cosy bars and a terraced garden with fine views over Norbury Park, it has much to recommend it. Not least the ales, Hogs Back TEA and Hop Garden Gold and Adnams and Badger Bitters.

The landlord is the chef and the menu is all on the blackboard. Snacks include jackets and ploughman's and a jumbo sausage in French bread. There are 4 vegetarian dishes, e.g. Thai green vegetable curry. There is a fine selection to suit both hungry walkers, like pan fried lambs' livers and bacon, home made seafood pie and steak and kidney pies, and the ladies who lunch, e.g. melon, prawn and avocado salad. Children under 12 are not allowed in the bars. A sign says "No dogs and no muddy boots". One dog without boots was in the garden but it might be wise to confirm current policy in advance.

The pub is open Mon-Sat from 11am-3pm and 6-11pm, Sun 12-3pm and 7-10.30pm. Food is served to 2pm lunchtimes.

Tel: 01372 372590.

The William IV is in Byttom Hill, an unsurfaced lane, reached by turning east off the A24 2½ miles north of Dorking at the Frascati Restaurant just north of the B2209, Old London Rd, signed to Mickleham. There is a small public car park in front of the Frascati, otherwise in Byttom Hill or School Lane.

Approx distance of walk 3½ miles. Start at OS Map Ref : TQ 174538.

A walk in woodlands and then across the glorious wild flower meadow atop Mickleham Down, where galloping horses may enhance the scene. Do this in July or August for the buddleia and butterflies or in October for the autumn colours. The final downhill stretch could be dangerously slippery after rain. The walk may be combined with Walk 24 at Point 2 and with Walk 17 from Point 3.

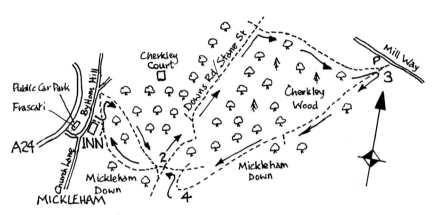

1. Take the footpath that runs uphill beside the pub. At a fingerpost turn L and with 2 gates ahead turn R at a fingerpost beside a third gate. Go gently uphill through woods and after passing a stile and barrier turn L on a crossing path.

2. The next crossing path is Downs Rd. If you turn R here for 350 yards you can combine with Walk 24 at Point 4, but for this walk turn L. At a 'T' junction turn L, still on Downs Rd, which at this point follows the line of the Roman Stane Street. To the L is the estate of Cherkley Court, former home of Lord Beaverbrook. The King William IV started life as a pub for the estate workers. At the top of a rise turn R at a fingerpost signed Mill Way. Keep on this path with a golf course to your L to reach a small car park.

3. This is Point 2 on Walk 17. Turn sharp R back into woods, now with a fence on your L. Pass a NT Mickleham Down sign on the R, step over a wire fence on the L and set out across the grass. Keep to the L of the fence as the RH side is used by horses. This area is covered in wild flowers attended by hosts of butterflies in season. A quick count gave us 12 species including clouded yellow, grayling, rare on chalk hills and, another rarity, the silver spotted skipper.

4. Pass a central bridleway waymark and keep to the R of a line of white posts. The track now bends sharp R into woods. At a crossing path turn L and at the next crossing path keep ahead. At a 3 path junction with a stile to the R keep ahead again, soon steeply downhill through buddleia bushes. At a fingerpost go over a crossing path and back down to the pub.

The Sportsman, Mogador.

The Sportsman is literally the end of the road on the southern edge of Walton Heath. Dating from the 1500s the name comes from its original use as a hunting lodge. It became an inn in the early 18th century and a stopping place for those paying, or evading, taxes on coal and other goods being brought into the Metropolitan area. Very cosy in winter, there are dining areas at both ends of the bar with a central fire. A lady at the next table summed it up perfectly. "In here you feel as if you could be on Exmoor".

The ales are Ruddles County, Wadsworth's 6X, Youngs' Special and Courage Best.

The extensive menu includes homemade soup, 5 jackets, 6 ploughman's and 6 salads, ham egg and chips, grilled gammon and sirloin steaks, cheese and asparagus in filo pastry. A daily specials board offers such as homemade curries, stuffed peppers with cheese topping, salmon and dill lasagne and giant Yorkshire filled with pork and cider casserole. Service is prompt and cheerful. There is a children's menu and the garden in equipped with a playground. Clean dogs on leads are welcome.

The pub opens at 10am daily for pre-walk coffees, with alcohol available on Mon-Fri 11am-3pm and 5.30-11pm; Sat 11am-11pm; Sun 12-10.30pm.

Tel: 01737 246655.

Mogador can be reached from Junction 8 of the M25 by turning north on the A217, then turning L into Stubbs Lane at the first roundabout. Cross Buckland Rd into Mogador Rd and the pub is at the very end of the tarmac road just after it turns sharp R. There is parking at the pub.

Approx distance of walk 4½ miles. Start at OS Map Ref : TQ 240532.

A breezy woodland and heathland walk on paths and bridleways some of which can be muddy in winter. It starts beside the famous Walton Heath golf course and continues into Walton on the Hill passing Mere Pond and turns back at The Bell, allowing combination with Walk 37. The return is over Banstead Heath where horse gallops may provide added interest. You may also combine with Walk 22 near the start – see text of para 1.

1. Turn L out of the pub and just before a 'T' junction turn R onto a signed bridleway. Maintain direction past a fingerpost and just past a notice board turn R, signed Walton on the Hill 1½ miles. (The notice board is Point 2 of Walk 22 for which you turn L.) The white posts denote the boundary of the Metropolitan area where from the mid 19th century, taxes were levied on certain goods, principally coal and wine, being brought into London. At a permissive ride waymark fork L beside the golf course. Ignore all paths off to the R until you reach a road, where cross over and follow the fingerpost on the R signed Mere Pond ½ mile. Go over a way-marked crossing path, pass the Blue Ball pub over to the L and reach Walton Rd.

2. Cross over and continue past Mere Pond on the track signed to The Bell (Walk 37). Just before the pub take the first footpath on the R signed to New Road. Go over several crossing paths and past a small pond. Cross a road and take the path beside the New Road sign. In a few yards fork R and keep on this path over several crossing paths. Pass a picnic seat on the L, go over a crossing path and past another picnic seat

and at the next major crossing bridleway turn L. Go over a crossing path and follow the fingerpost signed to Mill Road. Continue over several crossing paths and at Dorking Road, B2032, turn L up to a junction. Cross the road and take the signed bridleway next to Mill Road.

3. At a fingerpost bear half R, signed to Mogador. Note the sailless windmill to the R. Go over a crossing path and at a fork go L past a waymark post and downhill past 2 more posts. Go down a dip into woods and at a 4 fingered post bear half R signed Mogador 1½ miles. At a fork keep L on the main path that soon bends R and gets muddy for a short distance. Go over a major crossing path with a barrier to your L, now with woods on your L. The path bends L through the trees and at a permissive ride post turn R, now with the woods on your R. Continue beside the woods until they end at a crossing path with a 3 fingered post. Maintain direction here, veering slightly L to walk beside woods on your L. There is a parallel path just inside the trees. Continue to reach a notice board, where bear L back to the pub.

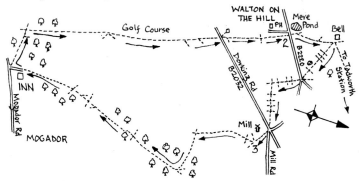

The Manor Hotel, Newlands Corner.

Given the hundreds who visit the Newlands Corner beauty spot daily come rain or shine, it is surprising that no proper pub was established here in the days when planning permission would not have been an issue. The Manor started life in 1890 as the country house of Lytton Strachey, a founder of the literary 'Bloomsbury Group' becoming a hotel in the 1920's. Squires Restaurant and Bar tacked on the side of the hotel is comfortable and nicely decorated with New Orleans prints and photographs of jazzmen, probably left over from when this was the popular venue for Sunday lunchtime jazz sessions.

Ales are limited to Old Speckled Hen and Guinness but there is an excellent wine list, with six available by the glass.

The 'cheffy' menu includes Croque Monsieur and Fettuccini Modo Nostra, but also some staples like beef and mushroom pie in Guinness, sausage and mash, American mixed grill "brunch", chicken and vegetable kormas and Caesar salad. If your visit coincides with a hotel function then sandwiches only may be available, so you would be wise to telephone in advance.

Lunchtime hours are 12-2.30pm with food service ending at 2pm, evenings 7-11pm. The bar is reached through the main hotel entrance, so they would prefer you to leave your boots in the boot.

Tel: 01483 222624.

The Manor Hotel is on the A25, 2 miles south of West Clandon and just north of the Newlands Corner car park on the North Downs, which you pass through in the middle of the walk. There is ample parking at both locations.

Approx distance of walk 5 miles (2¼ + 2¾). Start at OS Map Ref : TQ 045497.

The walk visits the popular beauty spot of Newlands Corner and takes in a stretch of the North Downs Way with fine views. Section 3 has masses of bluebells in season. Sections on the well used bridleways may be muddy. The walk may be combined with Walk 10 at point 4.

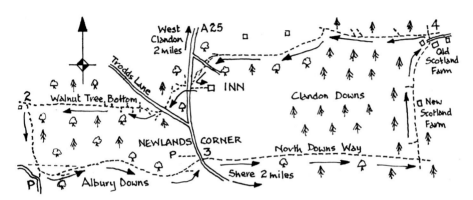

1. Walk down the hotel drive and turn R for 25 yards, then cross the road to a signed bridleway. Go forward, ignoring the immediate R turn and at a fork go L, then L again at a 'T' junction, passing some ancient yew trees. Cross Trodds Lane at a fingerpost and take the RH path opposite. Join another path coming in from the L and in a few yards at a fork keep L ahead past more fine yews. Ignore all side paths and go over crossing paths. This is Walnut Tree Bottom and in May 2004 the notice boards and all waymarks had been removed along here - so you must continue on the same path for ½ mile to reach a permanent point of reference.

2. With a wall ahead on the L, turn L on an unsigned bridleway steeply uphill. This levels out to a wide grass path then descends again to a waymarked crossing path. Go straight over and maintain direction over the next crossing path. In a few yards go diagonally L across a wide gravel track to a path sporting a 'Self Guided Trail' waymark. This curves L through a lovely patch of cowslips. Ignore a waymarked R turn and stay with this path as it curves uphill to join the N Downs Way at a waymark post. Follow this grass path keeping the trees to your L and enjoy the views. After passing 6

seats the path goes through a gap in bushes and curves L up to a seat in front of the car park. Keep to the R of the seat across grass to a ND Way fingerpost below the entrance to the car park. At this point you have the option to curtail the walk by turning L up the road past Trodds Lane back to the hotel and to do the second half after lunch.

3. Follow the ND Way direction across the A25 and past notice boards. Pass a viewpoint on the R and later 2 waymarks close together and a gate on your left. At the next waymarks where the signed path to the Silent Pool goes R, turn L and over a stile by a gate. The path soon widens to a track and you pass New Scotland Farm and descend on the grass path to Old Scotland Farm. A few yards into the farmyard at the second telegraph pole, bear L to a stile.

4. This is Point 3 on Walk 10. Do not cross the stile but turn L on the bridleway and keep on it ignoring all side paths for ½ mile. Continue when the path turns L uphill at a fingerpost passing farms on the R. After another ½ mile just past a field corner, fork L uphill into woods. At a fork keep L and cross a tarmac lane and the path winds R to reach the A25. Turn L and L again into the hotel drive.

The Fox Revived, Norwood Hill.

Just inside the door of The Fox Revived a stuffed fox sits in an armchair, glasses on, reading a volume from the pub's extensive library and holding a pewter tankard. You might think that this fox taking a reviver after eluding the local unspeakables gave the pub its name. In fact the more prosaic reason was a change of name in the 1950's from The Fox when the pub was reopened after a fire. Century old photographs are on view in the pub and another lasting reminder is Fred. If there is ever any disturbance to the happy atmosphere in the pub Fred, the ghost of an old cellarman who died of a heart attack in the cellar, may manifest himself in flying glasses and blasts of cold air at the same temperature as in the cellar. You have been warned. The staff still living are more welcoming and this spacious pub has 2 sunny conservatories, 2 open fires in winter and a large well maintained garden with fruit trees.

An open hatch allows you to watch the chefs at work and their concoctions include various baguettes, jackets, ploughman's and salads. Main courses are gammon steaks, smoked salmon fish cakes, scampi, chilli, chicken tikka, lasagne and vegetarian lasagne, steak and ale pie, pork and leek sausages and mash, etc.

The ales are London Pride and Adnams bitter, sometimes augmented by a guest.

The pub is open all day every day from 12 noon, food is served to 2pm Mon-Sat and 3pm Sun; evenings 7-9.30pm. Well behaved dogs on leads are welcome in the pub but children in the garden only.

Tel: 01293 863593.

Norwood Hill is situated midway between Leigh and Charlwood. It can be reached from the A25 east of Dorking via Brockham and Leigh and from the A217 at Hookwood by turning west on Horse Hill and then left on Collendean Lane. The pub is at the cross roads with Norwood Hill and has a large car park.

Approx distance of walk 4½ miles. Start at OS Map Ref : TQ 240436.

A walk mainly on farmland featuring flower meadows, an exotic bird and near the end a stunning bluebell wood in May. The walk may be combined with Walk 6 via a detour along Norwood Hill - see map.

1. Turn R out of the pub over the crossroads and down Norwood Hill Rd. Ahead you can see the traffic in and out of Gatwick Airport. After a bend in the road look for a stile in the hedge on the L. Cross a field diagonally L to a kissing gate and on over a stile and between a hedge and a wire fence. At the end of the fence turn R, then L through a gate and uphill on a grass path. We had brief sightings of a redstart and a cuckoo here. The path bends R briefly then continues uphill. Ignore a waymarked gate on the R and turn L up to a stile, then across a field to a road. Turn R for 100 yards, then L at a fingerpost. Go up the field beside the LH hedge. In May the fields on either side were a golden carpet of dandelions. Weeds they may be but en masse like this they can rival snowdrops or bluebells. Cross a stile, where we met a startled roe deer stag and bear slightly R across the next field to a stile in the fence. Follow the waymark half R and

down the next field and go between posts in the bottom corner. Pass some badger earth-works and keep beside the hedge on the R. Pass a gate, cross a stile and maintain direction up the field to a stile leading to a farm drive. It is worth detouring a few paces to the L to view Nutley Dean Farmhouse and pond.

2. Now turn R on the drive. At a fork keep R and maintain direction when the track narrows to a footpath. Pass a bluebell wood on the R and near the entrance to Ridgewood Stud you may see a peacock. It displayed on the path as we approached but then somewhat incongruously monitored our passing from the top of a manure heap. Pass a wooden barrier and turn L on a road. In 200 yards opposite South Lodge turn L over a stile. Take the wide track through a gate then bear half R to the bottom RH corner of the field. You may have to negotiate a fence built across the path in 2003 to reach

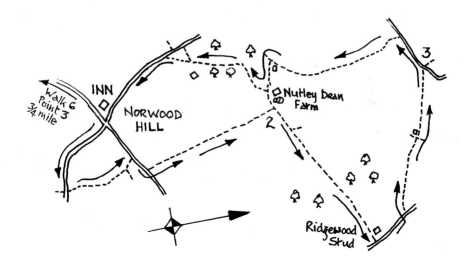

a waymarked footbridge and stile. Continue over the field to a stile by the gate in front of a house. Go over the house drive and to the R of a garage. Keep beside the hedge on the R to a stile. Cross a track and another stile, then go down through bluebells over a stile and through a patch of wild garlic. Cross a footbridge and head up a meadow passing between 2 power poles before bearing R and continuing beside a fence.

3. Cross a stile and turn L on a road. Pass 2 houses and turn L on a track at a fingerpost. Pass the nicely landscaped Greenings on the L, cross a footbridge and continue on a grass bridleway. This widens to become a track. Pass a house on the L and turn L through the gate to Nutley Dean Farm. Go up the drive and turn R before the entrance. In 40 yards turn R over a waymarked stile. Cross the field passing about 15 yards to the R of a rusty iron gate, then bear half R across the next field aiming for a stile in the centre of the woods ahead. Follow the path through this lovely bluebell wood and exit over a footbridge and stile. Bear half R across a field to a stile, cross a track and another stile, then cross the field diagonally to the bottom RH corner. Turn L on the road back to the pub.

Bluebell Wood, Norwood Hill

The Inn on the Green, Ockley.

There are 4 pubs on the busy A29 running through Ockley village. The spacious Inn on the Green, formerly a coaching inn and more recently The Red Lion, is the most conveniently sited for this walk.

They offer a warm welcome with 2 fires, Abbot ale, Bombardier, Greene King IPA and a choice of 6 wines by the glass.

The pub extends well back from the road frontage to an á la carte restaurant in a conservatory and a secluded garden with a play area beyond. Dogs are welcome everywhere except the restaurant. The bar menu features a choice of 4 meals for children as well as an excellent choice of baguettes, ploughmans, jackets, salads, vegetarian offerings and omelettes. More substantial fare includes dishes such as pan fried sea bass, calves liver and bacon, sausage and mash, crispy duck leg roasted in Burgundy and hoi-sin sauce, choice of stir fries, pork Normande, salmon and prawn bonne femme and beef forestière in a wild mushroom and Madeira sauce.

Opening hours are Mon–Thurs 11am-2.30pm and 5.30-11pm, Fri-Sat 11.30am-11pm, and Sun 12-10.30pm. Letting rooms are available on a room only basis.

Tel: 01306 711032.

Walk No. 29

The Inn on the Green is situated on the A29 in Ockley opposite the village green. The pub has a large car park.

Approx distance of walk 5½ miles. Start at OS Map Ref : TQ 148402.

A walk with views to Leith Hill over fields and bluebell woods to Forest Green and back. Mud could be a problem on bridleways in winter. There is a good chance of seeing deer. The walk may be combined with Walk 36 at Point 2 or Walk 14 at Point 3 to make longer rambles.

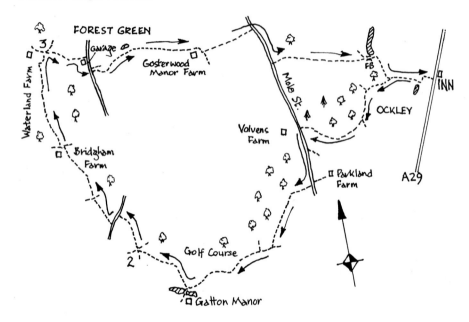

1. Turn L out of the pub and cross the road to a path across the village green. Turn L in front of No15, then R before the pond. Follow the path across a meadow to a fingerpost at the corner of a copse and turn L through the trees to a gate and footbridge. Go L at a fork and pass a stile on the L, then cross a footbridge. At a road, Mole St., turn L. After ¼ mile pass the drive to Parkland Farmhouse on the L and turn R at a fingerpost through woods and past a golf green. Maintain waymarked direction along the edge of the RH fairway passing a pond on your L. At a waymark post turn L, then bear half R following a fingerpost across 2 fairways to another fingerpost and into woods. Turn R on a gravel drive, cross a stile by a gate and bear R across a golf course bridge. Follow this track across the course until just before it passes between 2 ponds. Twenty yards before a wooden sleeper

bridge turn R beside the pond. The waymark post here may be hidden beneath a small oak tree. In a few yards a fingerpost directs you diagonally across the 9th fairway to a strip of woodland that runs between the 9th and the adjacent fairway. Maintain direction beside this fairway keeping the trees on your L. Pass 1 waymark post and at the second bear L on a path through the trees that emerges at a waymark opposite the ladies' 9th tee. Cross diagonally to a point just below the men's tee and continue through the next woodland strip to a fingerpost in front of the 5th green. Follow this between a bunker and the green to a path at the back of the green that leads out to a byway. Turn R here for a few yards to reach a 5 fingered post.

2. This is Point 3 on Walk 36. Go forward through a gate into a meadow and fork R ahead across to a stile and gate concealed in

bushes. Keep to the LH side of the field to 2 stiles and a road. Turn L for 25 yards, then R over a stile. Follow waymarks across a field, through a copse and over a footbridge, then along the LH edge of a field to 2 stiles. Maintain direction across a field to a stile and a gate. Continue with the waymarks along the RH side of 3 fields into Bridgham Farm. Go through a waymarked gate beside a garage and, after the next gate, bear half L to 2 stiles. Follow waymarks up 3 more fields and turn R over a stile by a gate onto a track.

3. At a concrete track with Waterland Farm to your L turn R. The next few yards to the stile are common to Walk 14 in reverse. As the lane bends L go forward to a stile, then bear half R across 2 fields and stiles to a

path beside sheds and out to a road. Turn R past Forest Green Garage, pass a footpath sign on the L and in a few yards take the signed bridleway on the L. Go through a gate and follow this drive for ¾ mile through Gosterwood Manor Farm with views L to Leith Hill. At a 'T' junction turn R on Mole St and, opposite Volvens Farm entrance, turn L into woods. At a fork keep R, cross a footbridge and turn R over a stile. Follow the fingerpost half L to a stile about 60 yards to the L of the far corner of the field and continue to a footbridge. Pass a pond on your L and bear R following the waymark to the corner of the copse. Take the second L at the fingerpost to cross the field on the path you started out on back to the village green and the pub.

Gatton Manor Grounds

The Punchbowl Inn, Okewood Hill.

Converted from a pair of 15th century cottages this attractive welcoming inn has a Horsham slab roof, a listed pig sty in the car park and tables on the front lawn. One of the 3 rooms is non-smoking and another houses a pool table and dartboard and a 'burger bar'. The main room has an inglenook fireplace decorated with horse brasses and with a log fire, exposed beams, polished flagstone floor and scrubbed pine tables.

Hall and Woodhouse owned they offer Tanglefoot and Badger ales with Gribble's Fursty Ferret as permanent guest. An earlier encounter with FF was at the Cyder House Inn, Shackleford (Walk No. 25 in Forty Walks in N Surrey) and it transpired that Phillip and Wendy Nisbet had migrated from there to the Punch Bowl. I hear that they also have designs on the nearby Scarlett Arms (Walk No.36). The natives hereabouts are most fortunate to be able to choose between two such excellent pubs.

As well as the homemade burgers their menu includes ciabatta sandwiches, Thai green curry along with steaks, fresh fish and imaginative vegetarian dishes in a comprehensive blackboard selection. A children's menu drawn by a young artist offers a choice of 5 dishes. Dogs are welcome.

The pub is open all day every day from 11am, 12 on Sunday. Food is served to 2.15pm Mon-Thurs and all day Fri-Sun.

Tel: 01306 627249.

Okewood Hill is 2 miles south of Ockley, signed from the A29. The Punch Bowl is in the centre of the village and has a large car park.

Approx distance of walk 4 miles. Start at OS Map Ref : TQ 133374.

A woodland and farmland walk on the Sussex border with good views in places, bluebells in season and the chance of seeing deer. The walk may be combined with Walk 36 at Point 2, Okewood Church. There may be mud in the woods in winter.

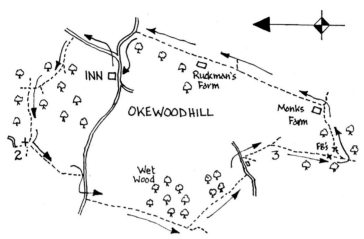

1. Turn L out of the pub and at a fork go L downhill. Opposite the Okewood Hill road sign turn L on a footpath into woods. At a waymarked fork keep R and at the next waymark take the wider central path. The path bends R, then you fork R to another waymark. Turn L here on a path that leads to a gate into the churchyard of St John The Baptist, Okewood. Described as "a gem in a perfect setting" it is certainly nice enough to visit twice – see also Walk 36.

2. With your back to the church porch turn L on the path towards the church hall. Just before the first tall conifer bear R to an old kissing gate and out to a waymarked path. Continue along a field edge and bear L on a tarmac drive past a gate to a road. Turn R for 200 yards and just before the first house on the L, turn L on a signed bridleway and through a 5 bar gate into Rosehill Farm. Continue through a metal gate and along the LH side of 2 fields. At a fingerpost maintain direction on a footpath to the L of a fence with Wetwood to your L, where you may see deer and bluebells in season. At a fingerpost at the end of the wood bear L to a stile in a fence. Turn R to another stile. Now head straight up a large field keeping close to the R of an island copse, then main-

tain direction to a concrete bridge and a waymark post. Bear half L across the next field to a stile by a metal gate. Turn L on a road, then R into the drive to Monks Farm.

3. Just before a gate turn R on a signed bridleway. Cross a small bridge and at an ancient fingerpost turn sharp L to another fingerpost and a sleeper bridge. More old fingerposts in close order lead you through a thicket to a wire fence corner. Follow the fingerpost between the fence and a hedge and you may see the Monks Farm Ladies Polo Team practising in the field on the R. Judging by the number of balls we threw back from the footpath loitering here could involve an element of risk. Go through a small gate and continue for a few more yards, then turn L at the next fingerpost. Go through a gate by the stable block and turn L on a farm road towards Monks Farmhouse then immediately R and out through a white gate onto a bridleway, the Sussex Border Path. Ignore side paths and the path goes uphill to another gate. Go straight on here on a tarmac drive past the imposing Ruckman's Farm and along a tree lined avenue to a road. Turn L back to the pub.

The Fox, Old Coulsdon.

From 1720 The Fox Alehouse was open at 5am to fill up the farm workers' bottles with home brewed ale as they passed by on their way to work. Now this is a large comfortable pub acquired by Vintage Inns in the 1990's and given their standard refurbishment. There are separate smoking and non-smoking areas and a high ceilinged baronial hall style central section with an open fire in winter. Outside is a patio packed with tables.

Our visit was in spring and the VI Spring Menu offered snacks including chicken Caesar wrap, smoked haddock melt, grilled rarebit muffins and grilled beefsteak sandwich. Among the main courses were beef and ale pie, chicken, leek and ham pie, hot chicken salad, gammon steak, Cajun chicken with bow tie pasta, baked sea bass and vegetarian specials: pumpkin risotto, red onion and potato tart and roast nut spinach and mushroom loaf. The children's menu included scampi and lemon chicken.

The ales are Bass and Tetleys. Given all the independent breweries in Surrey, Kent, Sussex and Hampshire producing excellent ales, you may deplore, as I do, the importation of these bland, mass produced mediocrities into the south east. If so you can always drink the wine. There are 10 to choose from, available by the glass, including the excellent Chilean Valdivieso, so no complaints there.

The pub is open all day every day from 11am, 12 on Sundays. Dogs are not allowed inside the pub.

Tel: 01883 330401.

The Fox is in Fox Lane, a turning off the B2030 Coulsdon Rd at Coulsdon Common, south of Old Coulsdon. From the M25 turn north on the A22 at Junction 6 and after 1 mile fork L on the B2030. Stay on this road for 2 miles through Caterham following signs for Coulsdon. Fox Lane is on your L. There is a large car park at the pub.

Approx distance of walk 4 miles. Start at OS Map Ref : TQ 318568.

A hilly walk on chalk downs through Happy Valley to Farthing Down and then to the lovely church at Chaldon with its fascinating wall paintings. There are bluebells and wood anemones in the woods and cowslips and butterflies on the grassy slopes. The walk could be combined with Walk 23 with a ½ mile detour from Point 3.

1. Turn L out of the pub along Fox Lane and at a fingerpost maintain direction on the tarmac, signed to Farthing Down. There is a parallel path in the wooded strip to the R and a series of exercise frames to keep the children amused on the L. At a signpost follow London Loop downhill and at the next signpost follow Farthing Down ¾ mile. The path runs along the side of Happy Valley and at a 3 fingered post in the woodland edge fork R, signed Drive Rd ½ mile. Go over a wide bridleway and fork L uphill through cowslips and past Post No 13. At a seat fork R and at a 'T' junction turn L on a chalk path with bushes on your R. Pass several seats placed to enjoy the lovely view, go over a crossing path and at a fork go L, keeping the bushes on your R. Go downhill and over a crossing path, now with a wire fence on your L. At the end of this enclosure fork L to a fingerpost signed Bridleway 742.

2. Turn L downhill here on the bridleway known as Drive Road. At a path junction in the valley bottom go straight on uphill

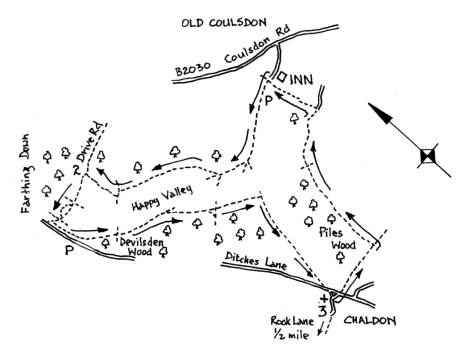

13th Century Wall Painting at St. Peter and St. Paul's, Chaldon

again. A less steep alternative (Bridleway 741) is signed on the R and the two meet again near the top. After 741 rejoins your path go over a crossing path and at a waymark post turn L on a permissive path. At another waymark post fork L on the grass keeping bushes on your L. Pass a Farthing Down notice and car park on your R and at a 3 fingered post go forward, signed Devilsden Wood/Happy Valley. Pass a 4 fingered post and follow Happy Valley and at a fork go L. With swathes of bluebells and wood anemones punctuated by patches of celandines, anything less like a devil's den than this wood would be hard to imagine. Perhaps the single patch of wild garlic holds a clue? At a fingerpost emerge onto the grass of Happy Valley and follow Chaldon Church, 1 mile. Keep close to the edge of the woods on the R to find a path and a fingerpost just inside the woods. Turn L at the fingerpost, cross a bridleway and emerge back on the grass, again with the woods on your R. Continue along the verge to a fingerpost in the corner and turn R, signed Chaldon Church ½ mile At a fingerpost bear half L across a field to the corner of a bluebell wood and continue downhill across the field. At the bottom go over a crossing track and on to Ditches Lane. Turn L then fork R to the Church of St Peter and St Paul, Chaldon. This special church, founded in Saxon times, has a famous wall painting dating from the 12th century called "Ladder of Salvation of the Human Soul" and other antiquities. Informative leaflets are available in the church which is normally open during daylight hours.

3. To combine with Walk 23 turn R out of the church and take the footpath on the L to Rook Lane – see maps. For this walk turn L out of the church gate and fork R down the road. At a fingerpost turn L, signed Piles Wood. Go up a field and on beside a bluebell wood on the L. At a 3 fingered post turn L, signed Happy Valley. Pass houses on the R and follow a fingerpost signed Happy Valley into woods. At a 4 fingered post in the bottom of the valley go straight on following Coulsdon Common ½ mile. The rough path goes uphill and at a fork keep R in the woods. At a tarmac road turn L past a metal gate and just before another gate turn R, then L onto a track. Reach Fox Lane opposite a notice board and turn R back to the pub.

The Bell, Outwood.

One of the finest pubs in Surrey and originally a coaching inn, The Bell dates from the late 17th century. The ceiling and wall timbers in the bar were taken from a Charles II Man o'War and the 5 cwt bell at the front was forged from melted down cannons of the same vintage. The pub also boasts an "authenticated" ghost of a 17th century lady, possibly connected to the presence in the rear garden of a hanging tree, used instead of a ducking stool hereabouts for the dispatching of witches.

The present Free House makes the best of the historic ambience featuring 2 fireplaces and scrubbed pine tables. The ales are Harvey's Sussex, Spitfire, Pedigree and a guest – Wicked Hound from the Somerset Cottage microbrewery on our visit.

The menu offers outstanding variety and quality with many home made dishes including soups, Brie parcels, steak and kidney pie, curries, chicken fajitas, vegetarian pasta bake, lasagne etc. Sandwiches and jackets are available and a choice of 20 baguette fillings. Examples from the daily specials board are pork and apple casserole, sea bass steak on ribbon vegetables, ½ lobster, crab mornay, oven roasted cod, lamb steaks, etc. Children and dogs are welcome and the small rear garden has a superb view if you don't mind the idea of dead witches waving in the breeze.

Hours are Mon-Sat 11am-11pm, Sun 12-10.30pm. Lunchtime food is served to 2pm and all day Sundays.

Tel: 01342 842989.

Walk No. 32

The Bell can be reached from the A25 by turning south at Bletchingly on Outwood Lane for 3 miles. There is ample parking at the pub or on Outwood Common (NT).

Approx distance of walk 4¼ miles. Start at OS Map Ref : TQ 328457.

You may be sidetracked at the start by the Outwood Windmill, dated 1665, the oldest working windmill in England. It is open Sundays between Easter and 31 October from 2-6pm. Tel : 01342 843458. The walk takes you through the lovely Hornecourt bluebell wood and across fields with superb views to Whitewood, continuing on farmland via the 12th century church at Horne. The walk may be combined with Walk 19 at Point 2.

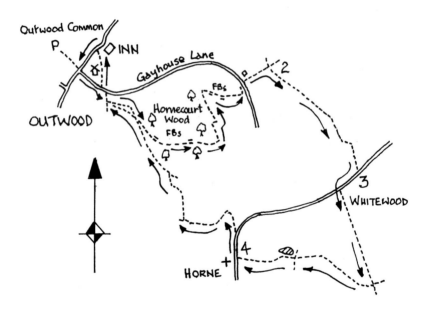

1. Turn L out of the pub past the windmill and turn L on Gayhouse Lane. In 100 yards just past a bungalow turn R on a track, then L over a stile into a field. The grass path ahead divides. Fork L to a hedge, then turn R along the hedge to enter Hornecourt Wood at the NT sign. Maintain direction downhill in the wood over a crossing path, down a dip and over a footbridge. The undulating path swings L, then at a waymark post turn L. At the next waymark turn R on a wide grass path, then L before a seat. Turn R over a waymarked footbridge, then another into a field. Turn R following the NT waymark along the hedge. At the bottom of the field turn L to a stile leading onto a road. Turn L, then immediately R on a track beside Horne Court Cottage.

2. At a waymarked crossing path turn R, cross a footbridge and a stile by a small pond. This section is common to Walk 19. Bear half L across a meadow to a footbridge and maintain direction over another meadow with fine views ahead. Follow the waymark across the next field, cross a footbridge and follow a fenced path. Turn R on a drive and at Whitewood Lane turn R away from Walk 19. In 150 yards turn L over a stile at a fingerpost. Follow the LH hedge to a stile at the bottom. Bear half R across the next field passing a central telegraph pole on your L, to a fenced grass path. There are pill boxes over to your L. Cross a stile and follow the waymark across the field to a stile in the bottom RH corner. Turn R to another stile and continue up the RH side of the

field. Ignore a footbridge on the R by another pill box and maintain direction over low barriers, then a crossing path and a stile. Pass a large pond, barely visible on the R and at the end of the field bear R to a stile and a footbridge. Turn L beside a school fence to a road, where cross to Horne church. St Mary's dates from the 13th century but only the south door and beams in the nave are original. The chancel has an interesting wall monument in carved and painted wood to John Goodwine and his wife dated 1618.

3. Turn L out of the church along the road. Just beyond the bend sign turn L through a kissing gate into a field. Keep beside the hedge on the L as it bends L and over a sleeper bridge, then turn L at a waymark. Follow the hedge round to a waymarked gap, where turn R still with the hedge on your L. At the next field corner bear half L across a field gap to a waymark and turn R, now with a hedge on your R. At the end of the field cross a concrete bridge into woods and turn L uphill. Pass a waymark post as you leave the woods and maintain direction along a field edge. Pass the NT notice on your R and continue beside the hedge and the windmill comes into view. Fork L on the grass to the stile and turn R, then L back onto Gayhouse Lane. Just past the bungalow on the L turn R on the grass, passing the windmill on your L and at the road turn R back to the pub.

Outwood Windmill

The Surrey Oaks, Parkgate.

Parts of this fine old favourite pub date back to 1570 but it was not until around 1850 that Mary Butcher, a wheelwright's widow, diversified into inn keeping with the inspired jingle "We'll put new wheels on your wagon while you are downing of a flagon."

Today Ken and Robyn Proctor are consistent winners of CAMRA Pub of the Year awards in Surrey and Sussex and feature in the Good Pub and Good Beer Guides. Resident ales are Adnams Southwold and Harveys Sussex and the array of pump clips testifies to the ever changing guest ales.

There are 2 bars one with an inglenook and a games room with a pool table, as well as a restaurant area. Bar snacks include 6 ploughman's, baguettes, ham, egg and chips, steak and kidney pudding and fried cod and scampi and the specials board offers such as roasted vegetables with feta cheese and sausage of the day, e.g. pork and orange, with mash and onion gravy. Children have a choice of 4 dishes and there is a play area in the garden.

Opening hours are Mon-Fri 11.30am-2.30pm and 5.30-11pm; Sat 11.30am-3pm and 6-11pm; Sun 12-3pm and 7-10.30pm. Last lunchtime orders are ¾ hour before closing and the kitchen is closed Sunday and Monday evenings.

Tel: 01306 631200.

The Surrey Oaks is in Parkgate Road about 1 mile NW of Newdigate. To reach the pub from the A24 south of Dorking turn east at Beare Green and follow signs for Newdigate and then Leigh. There is a large car park at the pub.

Approx distance of walk 4¾ miles. Start at OS Map Ref : TQ : 205436.

A flattish walk over farmland and through bluebell woods, mostly on sound bridleways but with some mud possible in the fields in Section 2.

1. Turn L out of the pub and opposite Broad Lane turn R over a stile. Turn L over the next stile and along the LH side of 2 fields to a road. Turn L for 25 yards, then turn R over a stile, then another into a bluebell wood. Go over a crossing path, then another following orange waymark arrows. Leave the woods over a stile and maintain direction up a large field to a stile about 50 yards to the R of farm buildings. At a second stile turn L towards the farm house, then bear half R to a stile by a gate.

2. Turn L on the farm drive and pause to admire the attractive Parkhouse farmhouse before turning R in front of it, soon to enter woods. Ignore a wooden gate on the L and keep ahead on a grassy path with a field on the R. Cross 2 stiles and a keep to the LH side of a long field. Cross 2 stiles and a small field to a metal gate. Keep to the RH side of a field, then beside a fence to a stile on the R. Cross onto the drive to Brook Farm and turn L and at the road cross over into Shellwood Road. At the top of a rise, opposite stables on the R, there is a fine view of Box Hill and the N Downs. In another 100 yards turn L on a concrete bridleway. Fork L before the gate to Shellwood Manor and between farm buildings. Continue on this long straight track for ¾ mile.

3. At a 'T' junction turn L for another ½ mile, then at a 'T' junction turn L and through an attractive group of houses including Ewood Old Farmhouse. You are now on a tarmac road until a 'T' junction, where turn R on Mill Lane. Pass Woodcote on the L and at a waymark post turn R on a footpath across a meadow. Turn L at a 'T' junction and continue through a tunnel of bushes. Fork R at a waymark post and turn L along a fence. Cross a road and continue on a fenced path through a bluebell wood to a road, where turn L back to the pub.

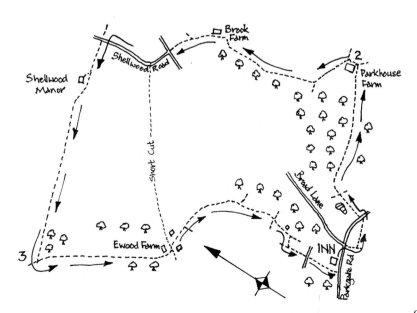

The Hurtwood Inn, Peaslake.

The Hurtwood Inn was built in 1920 on the site of 2 cottages, one a beerhouse. Now with 17 en-suite rooms and the integral 'Oscars' restaurant the inn is very popular with cyclists and walkers, the address in Walking Bottom clearly inspired by the demon hiker's threat "to walk your legs off." It was a delight to enter the comfortable bar in late October to be met by a cheering fire and Hogs Back TEA and Autumn Seer and Bateman's mixed grain brew Combined Harvest. There is also a good choice of wines by the glass.

The menu has sirloin and fillet steaks, pork chops, chicken curry, lasagne, Mediterranean salad and fresh fish dishes like Dover Sole and cod wrapped in Parma ham. Sandwiches are available and "speciality" sandwiches like salt beef mustard and dill, fresh crab and crème fraiche and dolcelatte and grapes. Children are welcome and there are tables outside at the front and on a side lawn.

The bar is open Mon-Fri from 11am-3pm and 5.30-11pm and all day weekends. Lunch is served to 2.30pm.

Tel: 01306 730851.

The Hurtwood Inn is in the centre of Peaslake. Follow signs from the A25 via Shere. Parking is at the pub or in 2 free car parks on the walk – see map.

Approx distance of walk 4⅓ miles. Start at OS Map Ref : TQ 086448.

You may hurt by the time you reach the top of Pitch Hill or you may have swallowed some hurts, that being the local name for the small tasty blueberries or bilberries that grow hereabouts. The walk starts on farmland with views to the N Downs and explores the Winterfold Forest and the Hurtwood. Best done in the autumn for the colours and the sweet chestnuts. The walk may be combined with Walk 13 at the Ewhurst windmill in Section 2.

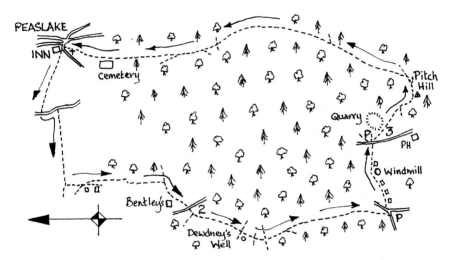

1. Turn R out of the inn and immediately R again onto a footpath uphill. Maintain direction between fields to join a gravel drive, then turn L on a road. In 100 yards turn R at a bridleway fingerpost. After the third gate which is in a dip, turn immediately L with a hedge on your L. Go through another gate and in a few yards turn L on a signed footpath, then fork R beside gardens. Bear R at a waymark post and turn L before the rear entrance to the Bentley Copse Scout Camp. The path runs parallel to the earth boundary. At the next waymarked crossing bridleway turn R, soon passing the main entrance to the camp, where maintain direction on the drive.

2. Cross a road to the drive opposite and in 15 yards fork L at a fingerpost. Ignore a L fork and go downhill through a gate and over a crossing path, passing Dewdney's Well on your R. Continue over a wide gravel track and uphill on another wide forest track. At a fork keep L, still uphill. Pass a newly excavated pond and maintain direc-

tion to go through a small gate and on to reach a road opposite HC Car Park No. 4. Turn L to a cycleway post, then cross the road to a fingerpost and continue past houses on your R. Bear R round the Ewhurst windmill and join a path beside Four Winds. Go steeply downhill and out through a gate. The Windmill (Walk 13) is down to your R. Cross the road to the entrance to HC Car Park No.3.

3. Take the path on the R between 2 low posts going uphill past a quarry on the L. Pass the OS Trig Point at the top of Pitch Hill and admire the views. Keep ahead for 60 yards to a Greensand Way waymark post and turn L. There are more fine views and at a fork keep R to pass a metal seat. In 50 yards fork L on a wide path. Stay on this over 3 crossing paths, then at a 'T' junction turn L on a wide track. At the next fork keep R ahead to pass a cemetery on the L. At a waymark post fork R downhill on a rough narrow path to reach St Mark's Church and the inn.

Skimmington Castle, Reigate Heath.

This pub is a bit special and it is no surprise to find it featured in the Good Pub Guide. Hidden away on the heath it was once the haunt of highwaymen. From the outside it is an attractive building with tables on the front patio with good views all round. Inside there is a long front room with a small bar at one end and a servery to the side leading to 3 more rooms in the original farmhouse part of the building, which is over 200 years old. The main room has a superb working inglenook fireplace – (see lower picture on page 98). There is a room for non-smokers downstairs.

Deservedly popular, at 1pm on a Wednesday in February we could not find 2 seats together, so we sped around the second half of the walk just in time to beat the 2pm deadline for main course food. It was well worth coming back for – Thai chicken curry and prawn and salmon salad to rank with the best. The menu, all on blackboards, includes jackets, ploughman's and sandwiches, main courses like fish pie, medallions of pork, breast of duck, roasted vegetable lasagne and vegetable tagliatelli. Another board of chef's specials had Chinese chicken stir fry, plaice filled with spinach and mushrooms, sardine salad and mushroom Strogonoff.

Pubmaster owned, the ales are Old Speckled Hen, Young's Special, Adnams Bitter and a guest e.g. Adnams Broadside. There is a choice of 8 wines by the glass. Dogs are welcome in the bar, children and mobile phones in the garden only.

Hours are Mon-Sat 11am-3pm and 5.30 (Sat 6pm)- 11pm, Sun 12-10.30pm.

Tel: 01737 243100.

Skimmington is reached by turning south off the A25 into Flanchford Rd, ½ mile west of Reigate. Pass a car park on the L and turn L into Bonny's Rd. The pub is at the end of this humpy track and there is a large car park at the rear.

Approx distance of walk 5 miles (2½ + 2½). Start at OS Map Ref : TQ 237497.

A varied walk that returns to the pub halfway, giving the option of two short walks. Mainly on the Greensand Way the walk visits a windmill with a surprise interior and crosses farmland to a pretty millpond. The second half is through woodland and across the top of Reigate Park with fine views.

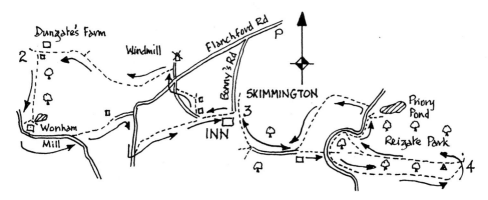

1. Turn sharp L out of the pub to a Greensand Way (GW) marker post and follow the path to a lane, where turn R across the front of Tile House to another GW marker. Go into woods with gardens to your R, then opposite the last house turn L back to the lane. Turn R and cross a road to the entrance to Reigate Heath Golf Club. Go up the drive to the windmill. The key is available on request at the Club House. Retrace your steps down the drive to a GW post and turn R on a path. Maintain direction across a golf fairway to another post and a path to the L of a white cottage. Follow the GW between fields, then through a field, then fork L with a stream on your R. Cross a bridge and approach Dungates Farm, where you may be greeted by 7 friendly dogs.
2. In the farmyard turn L past The Granary onto a track leading to a stile. Maintain direction along the RH side of a field and over a double stile. Cross the next field diagonally to the bottom LH Corner and cross a stile beside the pretty Wonham Mill pond. Turn R to the road. Turn L past the mill and where the road bends R fork L on a signed bridleway uphill, then down to join a lane. At a 'T' junction turn R on the road and at the top of a hill turn sharp L at a fingerpost onto a path. Follow this between fences and over 2 drives, passing Tile House on your left and back to the pub.
3. Pass across the front of the pub to a fingerpost and turn R on the GW uphill, then down to a junction of paths. Turn L on the surfaced lane. Cross a bridge and pass houses on the R and continue uphill. Cross Littleton Lane and go up steps (GW) to a crossing path, where turn R off the GW. Continue around the edge of a wood soon with fine views to the R. This is Reigate Park. After ½ mile pass gardens on the R and the path curves L to a junction of paths.
4. Turn sharp L uphill following the GW waymark. Pass to the L of a stone seat and a trig point to join a wide grass hilltop path. Where the grass ends fork R downhill into woods. At a 'T' junction turn R and at a fork with a house roof to your L go L steeply down to a road. Over to your R is Priory Pond, usually worth a visit for bird watchers, but to continue the walk turn R down the road for 75 yards to a fingerpost on the L. Follow this path with a stream on the R. Go through a kissing gate, then over a stile and on to another that leads out to the lane you were on earlier. Turn R and retrace your steps over the bridge and take the RH bridleway back to the pub.

Skimmington Windmill

Inglenook fireplace, Skimmington Castle

The Scarlett Arms, Wallis Wood.

Tim in the Wheatsheaf at Ewell told us about the outstanding Scarlett Arms and we are indebted to him for this CAMRA award winning addition to our list of special pubs.

Under new management in 2004, this Hall and Woodhouse pub started life as two cottages. It still has the two front doors and as you enter you could be stepping back a century or more. The small rooms include one with a coal fire that could be your Granny's parlour. The main bar has a lovely fireplace at one end where, on our visit, a couple of tree trunks were smouldering – (see upper picture on page 101). Dogs and children are welcome and children can have small portions of most main meals.

Ales available are Badger, Fursty Ferret and Sussex.

The menu features ciabattas or sandwiches, five salads and three ploughman's, tagliatelli, lasagne, scampi, whitebait, steaks and oysters, gammon, superb home baked ham, egg and chips. Specials include dishes such as baked cod with pesto crust, chicken supreme with port and garlic, stir fried sirloin steak and beef Madras. The pleasant front garden is very popular in summer.

Opening hours are Mon-Sat 11am-2.30pm and 5.30-11pm and Sun 12-3pm and 7-10.30pm. There is no food on Mondays.

Tel: 01306 627243.

Walk No. 36

Wallis Wood is situated about 3 miles SW of Ockley and is signed from the A29 or from the Horsham Road 2 miles SE of Ewhurst. The Scarlett Arms is in Walliswood Green Road. There is ample parking opposite the pub.

Approx distance of walk 4½ miles. Start at OS Map Ref : TQ 119382.

A lovely walk with bluebells in season and extra colour in autumn in beech and oak woods. There are deer in the woods, fine views to the N Downs, an old church and other interesting property. The walk may be combined with Walk 30 at Point 2 and Walk 29 at Point 3.

1. Turn L out of the pub and in 50 yards L through a kissing gate. Go straight on at a 4 fingered post, go over a waymarked crossing path and turn L at the next waymark beside 2 gates. At a waymarked fork go R and soon downhill with a stream down to your R. Cross one footbridge and bear R to another and up steps to the gate to St John the Baptist Church, Okewood.

2. This is Point 2 of Walk 30. The lovely church in an equally fine setting with a mulberry tree near the front door, dates from 1220. The remnants of 13th century wall paintings are still visible. One 16th century priest was blessed with a name straight out of the Goon Show. Sir Hamlett Slynge would have been a worthy confessor for Moriarty, Bloodnock and Hercules Grytpype Thynne. Retrace your steps to the nearest footbridge and in a few yards turn L, then R past a waymarked post and over another footbridge. Go up and along the bank to a stile, keep to the LH side of a field to another stile and on through a smallholding with turkeys, geese and guinea fowl. Maintain direction over a footbridge and turn L on a lane opposite the entrance to Gatton Manor. In 60 yards turn R in front of Okewood Cottage and at the second fingerpost take the Public Byway ahead. Stay on this path for ½ mile to reach a 'T' junction with a 5 fingered post.

3. This is Point 2 of Walk 29. Turn L, still on the Byway, and at Mayes Green turn R round a kidney shaped pond onto a road. Pass the Grade 1 listed Shoes Farm with fine views ahead to Leith Hill. At a fingerpost turn L over a waymarked stile and straight

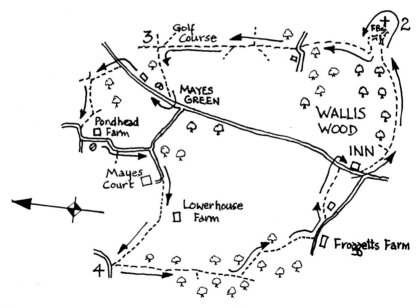

across a field to a fingerpost and into a blue-bell wood, then over a footbridge. Cross another stile and keep to the LH side of a field. Turn L in front of the next stile, then cross another stile on the R. Keep L, then bear R to a gate and across another field to a gate onto a lane. Turn L passing Pondhead Farm, another lovely setting. Ignore a fingerpost on the L and turn R at the next one on the R, signed Mayes Court. When the drive bends R go ahead to a stile and a fenced path with views of Holmbury Hill. Go through a gate and across a field to a stile, then turn R on the drive of Lower Farm.

4. At a fingerpost at the end of the drive turn L on a Byway. After ½ mile turn L over a stile into woods. Cross a sleeper bridge and a stile into a field. Maintain direction over 3 more stiles and turn R on the drive to Northlands. Look back for a view of yet another fine house. At a road turn L, then L again into the waymarked gate of Walliswood Farm. Keep to the L of the buildings and cross a field via 2 stiles, then out through a kissing gate. Advance to the road and turn R back to the pub.

Okewood Church, Walliswood

The Bell, Walton on the Hill.

The Bell is a tiny very welcoming local with a central bar and two fires in winter. It is packed with bric a brac and even a piano. The pub straddles the border between Walton on the Hill and Tadworth. It must be swamped annually by the large number of walkers who come this way on Derby Day. The address is Withybed Corner and in winter the few tables on the grass outside seem to be in danger from the encroaching withybed that doubles as a duck pond. Because it is so small children are not allowed inside the pub and dogs on a lead only.

The ales are Flowers IPA, London Pride and Bass with a guest, e.g. Burton's 1744, and there is a choice of wines by the glass.

The menu is excellent value using quality produce – try the ham off the bone and offers soup, sandwiches and jackets, steak baguette, ploughmans, ham egg and chips, home made quiche, delicious home made curry of the day and daily blackboard specials. Having watched the amount of TLC the landlady lavished on her pot plants you can be sure that similar care goes into the food preparation.

Hours are Mon–Fri 12-3pm and 5.30-11pm, Sat and Sun open all day from 12 noon. N.B.1 No food on Sundays and Mondays. N.B.2 If you are going mob handed it would be sensible to book in advance.

Tel: 01737 812132.

The Bell is hidden away in Withybed corner at the edge of the common between Tadworth and Walton on the Hill. It can be reached by footpaths (about 750 yards) from Tadworth Station or the walk may be started from Tattenham Corner Station – see map. By car turn west off the A217 onto the B2220,Tadworth St, and in 1 mile turn R before Mere Pond where the pub is signed. There is limited parking at the pub.

Approx distance of walk 4½ miles. Start at OS Map Ref : TQ 227557.

A walk over Walton and Epsom Downs with fine views and the added interest of horse gallops and Epsom Race Course. The walk may be combined with Walk 26 at the start. As the walk crosses the race course race days are best avoided.

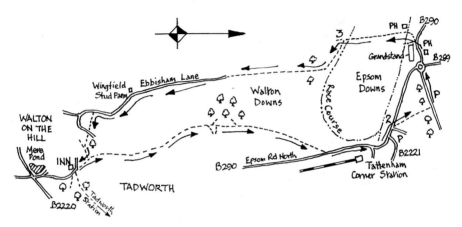

1. Turn L out of the pub, pass a barrier and a white coal tax post and fork R on a footpath. At a 'T' junction turn R on a lane and at a fingerpost fork L signed Epsom Lane North 1¼ m. This long downhill path runs between hedges with good views to the L. At a waymark fork L and at a noticeboard fork R. At the next fork follow Epsom Lane North ½ m. At a 'T' junction turn R on a wide track and listen out for skylarks. At a 'Racehorses Only' sign cross the B290 and turn L on the pavement. Cross the end of Tattenham Cres. Tattenham Corner Station is on the R. Continue on the grass and over the other end of Tattenham Cres. Pass a car park and cross Old London Rd.
2. In 15 yards fork R on a path and through woods to Grandstand Rd, where turn L along the grass verge. There is a fine view on the R, shame about the gasometer. Bear L round the roundabout and take the B290 signed to Epsom passing the grandstand on your L. At a traffic light turn L, then bear R along the rails. At a fork turn L across the

racecourse to pass The Rubbing House pub, once an excellent venue with much racing memorabilia but sadly closed in 2003. Take the road from the pub signed Walton Downs ¾ mile. In 50 yards fork R off the road past a metal barrier and in a few yards fork L down hill on grass then up again. Pass a red X marker post and at a fork keep ahead L. Cross a road, then the racecourse.
3. Turn L along the rails and at a Caution notice turn R on a crossing path through woods. At a 'T' junction go over the crossing path and maintain direction over grass to pass a notice board and then on over gallops and down hill on a faint path. Cross gallops protected by white barriers and go ahead on a track past a barrier and notice board. This is Ebbisham Lane and you stay on this for ¾ mile. At a fingerpost past Wildwoods Riding Centre turn L on a footpath between fences with good views to the L. Cross a road and a stile. After the next stile turn L, then at a fingerpost turn R back to the pub.

The Stepping Stones, Westhumble.

In Surrey and Hampshire you are unlikely to find a better 'Best' than Ringwood's. To find it in the company of Abbot, Spitfire, Old Speckled Hen and London Pride reveals a rare discernment. The same sentiments might apply to the excellent choice of wines by the glass.

This spacious comfortable pub, refurbished in 2003, is very popular with cyclists and walkers and is often the first and/or last stop for those using Box Hill and Westhumble Station.

The pub offers a comprehensive snack menu of sandwiches, soup, jackets, baguettes and Welsh rarebit with main courses like chicken tikka masala, liver and bacon and braised gammon with mustard sauce. The specials board features salads and a choice of roasts and novelties like smoked haddock and spring onion fishcakes.

Children are welcome in the dining area and garden and child's portions of some main courses are available. Dogs in the garden only, where a water bowl is supplied.

The pub is open Mon-Sat from 12-3pm and 5-11pm, Sundays 10.30pm.

Tel: 01306 889932.

Westhumble is reached by turning west off the A24 1 mile north of Dorking. The pub is situated between the A24 and Box Hill and Westhumble railway station. There is parking at the pub and at 2 public car parks en route – see map.

Approx distance of walk 5¾ miles. Start at OS Map Ref : TQ 170517.

The walk may be combined with Walk 24 as that walk passes the Stepping Stones and with Walks 9 and 16 as all three pass through Point 2.
A favourite walk with many fine views, a section in beech woods and another along the bank of the R. Mole with the chance of seeing kingfishers.

1. Turn L out of the pub past Box Hill and Westhumble Station and over the railway bridge. Fork R to pass the quaint Westhumble Chapel onto Crabtree Lane that soon gives nice views to the R over Mickleham and Norbury Park. After ½ mile pass a car park and the views are now to the L. Ranmore Church spire on the horizon is where you are headed. At the end of the lane take the path to the R of No. 3 Crabtree Cottages, signed to Ranmore. At a fork behind the cottage keep R ahead for ¼ mile in the wooded strip between fields. At a waymark post before a stile turn L downhill and in a few yards at a fork keep ahead R. Ignore side paths and cross the edge of a field via 2 gates.
2. Cross Chapel Lane to the bridleway opposite. This is Point 2 on both Walks 9 and 16.

Pass a National Trust sign and at a fork keep ahead uphill soon to enter Dorking Wood. At a fork keep ahead R through predominantly beech woods for ¾ mile to emerge opposite St Barnabus Church, Ranmore Common. Turn L beside the tarmac on the N Downs Way. By the entrance to Denbies continue forward on the concrete track and at a finger post turn R signed N Downs Way.
3. At the next junction turn L and soon enjoy superb views over the vineyard to Dorking and beyond. The vineyard is the largest in England and offers tours by roadtrain and wine tastings, Tel 01306 876616. The track bends L giving views of Box Hill, then descends over a crossing path. At a waymark post go L off the road and in 20 yards fork R signed N Downs Way.

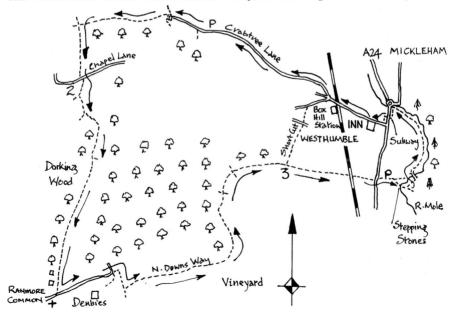

105

Walk No. 38

At the next fingerpost if you are running late or getting thirsty you could shorten the walk by ½ mile by turning L on a signed footpath to Westhumble – see map. Otherwise continue down to a waymarked gate and under the railway arch. Turn L briefly at the A24 then cross the road and go through the car park. Fork R to cross the stepping stones over the R Mole that gave the pub its name and turn L beside the river. Re–cross the river by the bridge and turn R along the bank. [If the water level is high the stepping stones may be submerged. In this case return to the car park and take the path signed to the bridge. Pass the footbridge on your R and continue along the bank as above.] You might be lucky enough to see a kingfisher as there are frequent sightings here. At Burford Bridge turn L and cross the road by the subway then turn L and R back to the pub.

Stepping Stones Across the River Mole

The Star, Witley.

The white painted rendered exterior of the Star conceals its age which is revealed by the interior beams. With long traditions as a village local it is nicely laid out and comfortable with two bars and a dining extension at the back. The sunny garden also has a rear section ideal for families where there is a slide and swings. Children are further encouraged with a choice of five dishes on a children's menu.

For adults there are jackets, baguettes and sandwiches with a wide range of fillings and home made pizzas with French bread base or thin crust and a choice of 7 toppings. Sausages and mash is another speciality. Choose from 8 sausages including beef and Guinness, spicy Mexican pork and wild boar and calvados, and 4 different gravies. Also available are sirloin and gammon steaks, chicken, ham and broccoli pie, steak, mushroom and ale pie, curry of the day, etc.

The ales are Pedigree and Greene King IPA with a guest, e.g. Jennings Cumberland or Hook Norton Old Hookey. Dogs are welcome.

Opening hours are Mon-Thurs 11.30am-3.30pm and 4.30-11pm; Fri-Sat 11am-11pm and Sun 12-3pm and 7-10.30pm.

Tel: 01428 684656.

Walk No. 39

The Star is on the A286 Petworth Rd on the northern edge of Witley. There is parking in front of the pub.

Approx distance of walk 6 miles, or 5 miles taking a short cut. Start at OS Map Ref : SU 946406.

This is a lovely walk in Springtime. The fields around Tuesley are a stronghold for skylarks and the many little streams have banks covered in celandines and daffodils. Later there are bluebells in the woods. The full walk visits a shrine to a 7th century church.

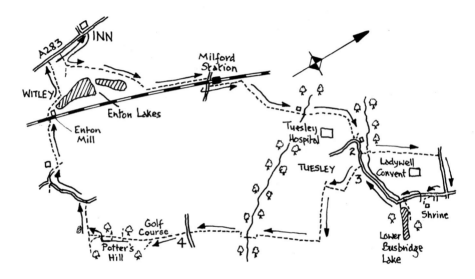

1. Turn R out of the pub and turn L at a sign for Enton Lakes. Fork L on a track at a waymarked telegraph pole and pass Lower Enton Lake on the R. Public access is denied but we glimpsed a heron and a pair of white fronted geese through the vegetation. Cross a stream twice, pass a bamboo grove and bear L beside the railway line. At Milford Station cross the line and bear L through the car park to a fingerpost and down Summer Lane. The skylark chorus should begin here. Just past a house on the L, where the lane bends R, go ahead on a waymarked path. Cross a stream, pass the boarded up Tuesley Hospital and at a waymark bear R across a sports field to a fingerpost in the corner. Turn L on a road past Crowts and down hill.

2. There is a fingerpost on the L next to Tuesley Manor Cottage. You can shorten the walk by 1 mile here by continuing along the road to the next fingerpost on the R and following para 3. For the full walk turn L here downhill on a path and cross a stream and up steps. Continue between fences. Ladywell Farm is to the L and Ladywell Convent to the R. At a road turn R past the convent entrance to a crossroads where turn R into Tuesley Lane. Pass Minster Rd and fork L at a fingerpost through a kissing gate. The Ladywell Shrine is to the L. Access to the small enclosure is restricted but it can be seen perfectly well from outside. The 7th Century church on this site was the first Christian church in the area and was mentioned in the Domesday Book. Retrace your steps and turn L back on the road. [At the bottom of the hill at a fingerpost on the L a footpath leads to Busbridge Lakes, if you have time for further exploration.] The road crosses then runs beside a stream. Pass Tuesley Manor and in 40 yards on the L reach the fingerpost referred to in the second sentence of this para.

3. Turn up steps to a stile and continue along the top of a bank between fields. The skylarks should be here again – we counted 7 in the next mile – but their days may be numbered as there are plans to cover these fields in polytunnels for a strawberry farm in 2004/5. Turn R at a stile and along a fence to another stile. Turn L at the finger-post on a farm track between vast open fields. At a fingerpost turn R and before woods go L then R at fingerposts to pass through a bluebell copse. On the other side go R then L to resume the original line, passing beside a power pole on your L. Cross a stile and continue on a fenced path to a road.
4. Cross the road and maintain direction down a drive and past a tennis court, then between hedges beside a golf course. Go over a crossing path and at a path junction on the golf course cross to a 'Please Use Path' notice and turn R. Bear L uphill through bluebells passing 3 waymark posts on your R. At the next waymark fork R down hill through trees and follow the waymark down across a golf fairway to a waymarked crossing track, where turn R. At a road turn L uphill and at a junction turn R at a fingerpost on an unmade road. Pass Great Enton and turn L downhill and under a railway arch. Bear L between the mill pond and Enton Mill. Turn R past the mill and continue beside the mill stream to the A283, where turn R back to the pub.

Ladywell Shrine

The Grantley Arms, Wonersh.

The Grantley Arms, formerly The Fighting Cocks, is an impressive old established inn, exhibiting exposed beams and a skittle alley and hidden away an old bakery only used for private functions. Dating from the mid 18th century it was renamed after Lord Grantley, a prominent local in the 19th century. One Lord Grantley is said to have lost the pub to a servant in a poker game. The pub was reputedly haunted by a monk for a time until an Irish barmaid, fed up with the manifestations, performed a successful 'exorcism'. I cannot quote what she said but if you watch Roy Keane's lips next time he is sent off for 'intent to maim' you will get the general idea.

In those days the landlord brewed his own ales. Now the excellent selection includes their own Grantley Arms, brewed by Hogs Back, with 3 constantly changing guests from a list of 60, e.g. Fursty Ferret, Tanglefoot, Spitfire, Gales HSB.

The menu offers an outstanding selection of bar meals : sandwiches plain and toasted, including a triple decker, a choice of 13 oven baked jackets, 11 baguettes and 5 ploughman's, various sausages with assorted flavours of mashed potatoes, all day breakfast and vegetarian breakfast. The children's choices also include vegetarian sausage. An equally extensive specials board makes this a pub where there will be something to suit even your most pernickety maiden aunt. Our experience in June 2004 was that it was all beautifully cooked and presented.

The pub is open from 12-2.30pm and 6-11pm Mon-Sat and 12-10.30pm Sunday. Lunchtime food is served to 2pm. Dogs are not allowed inside the pub but there are tables out front and in a rear 'suntrap' courtyard.

Tel: 01483 893551.

Wonersh is situated about 3 miles SE of Guildford between Shalford and Shamley Green. The Grantley Arms is on the B2128 in the centre of the village. There is ample parking at the pub.

Approx distance of walk 4¼ miles. Start at OS Map Ref : TQ 017452.

A regular winner of Best Kept Village awards Wonersh is still attractive in spite of the constant through traffic. This walk explores the Great Tangley Manor estate and Tangley and Chinthurst hills. There are fine views, much bird song, bluebells and chestnuts in season. Nettles in Section 1 prohibit the wearing of shorts after the end of April.

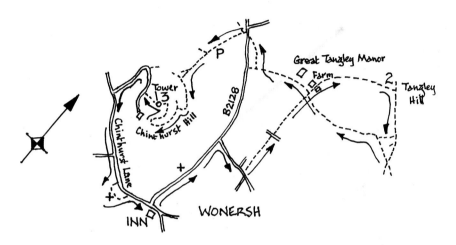

1. Cross the road from the pub to the Village Stores and turn R up the B2128, passing the village green and the United Reform Church with 2 spires. Chinthurst Hill rises behind the church. Turn R into Blackheath Lane and just before Barnett Lane go up steps next to a phone box on the L. Follow this narrow footpath to a kissing gate, where turn L then R at a fingerpost. There are nice views of the N Downs and St Martha's hill top church ahead. At Great Tangley Manor Farm you could shorten the walk by 1 mile by turning L – see map. Otherwise maintain direction past the farm buildings, one a tithe barn. The track narrows and curves R to a cottage. Turn R between fences here and up Tangley Hill. At 2 forks keep ahead L to reach a fingerpost by a double gate.
2. Turn sharp R and like the G.O. Duke of York's men march back down the hill again, through bluebells in season. Back at the farm maintain direction down the drive, soon passing the entrance to Great Tangley

Manor. We were surprised here by a close view of a female blackcap, or browncap to be precise, singing. A bit scratchy but nice enough. One wonders how she is viewed in warbler society. With contempt as a whistling woman or a crowing hen or as an innovator and potential duettist with her accomplished mate? Something to muse upon before turning R at a Downs Link fingerpost. Cross a road and continue on the Downs Link. At a fork keep L, pass a pond and a small car park on the L and at a fingerpost keep L ahead. At a fork before steps go L and in 20 yards turn L on a crossing path that circles Chinthurst Hill through more bluebells. At a 'T' junction turn L and there is a fine view over Wonersh. Ignore a turning on the R and continue on this path as it swings round to the R and up to the tower. This folly was built in 1935 by a former landowner but is boarded up now.
3. After admiring the views and the rhododendrons stand with your back to the tower on the opposite side to the black door, then

111

go forward over a grass path to a wider grass 'fairway'. Turn L and after 150 yards with a large house over to your L bear half R down to a tarmac drive. Turn R and follow it round a hairpin bend and down to a 'T' junction. Turn L on Chinthurst Lane and L again at the main road. Turn R into the church gate, then L in front of the church and follow the path across the green to exit through an arch. Turn R on the road back to the pub.

Great Tangley Manor Farm

Chinthurst Hill